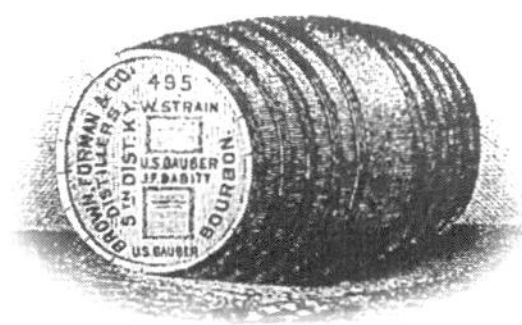
BROWN, FORMAN & CO.
DISTILLERS
5TH DIST. KY.
495
W. STRAIN
U.S. GAUGER
J.F. DABITT
U.S. GAUGER
BOURBON.

True Bluegrass Stories

History from the Heart of Kentucky

Tom Stephens

Foreword by Stephen M. Vest, *Kentucky Monthly*

The History Press

Published by The History Press
Charleston, SC 29403
www.historypress.net

Cover: painting by Paul Sawyier. *Courtesy of Paul Sawyier Art Gallery, Frankfort, KY.*
www.paulsawyierartgallery.com

First published 2008

Manufactured in the United States.

ISBN 978.1.59629.545.2

Library of Congress Cataloging-in-Publication Data

Stephens, Tom (Thomas E.)
True Bluegrass stories: history from the heart of Kentucky / Tom Stephens.
p. cm.
ISBN 978-1-59629-545-2
1. Bluegrass Region (Ky.)--History--Anecdotes. 2. Bluegrass Region (Ky.)--Social life and customs--Anecdotes. 3. Bluegrass Region (Ky.)--Biography--Anecdotes. 4. Kentucky--History--Anecdotes. 5. Kentucky--Social life and customs--Anecdotes. 6. Kentucky--Biography--Anecdotes. I. Title.
F457.B6S74 2008
976.9'3--dc22
2008025947

To Gene and Leslie

Contents

Foreword

Kentucky Monthly is a contemporary magazine about the Kentucky of today, but no one can have a full understanding of the way things are without knowing the background, the history behind the traditions that make the commonwealth unique.

Few people have the wealth of knowledge and also the storytelling ability of Tom Stephens, who has written *Kentucky Monthly*'s "Looking Back" section since its inception in September 1998. His stories span a broad breadth of interest and people, and Tom is equally at ease discussing the days following the American Revolution as he is the 1970s, the interesting era when we, then junior-high students, first met.

Several of the stories featured in this collection have garnered state and regional awards, and all have been praised by *Kentucky Monthly*'s loyal readers, who often call the magazine's Frankfort offices asking for more.

If this is your first opportunity to read Tom's stories, you're in for a real treat. If you are, like us, revisiting these opportunities to "look back," I can assure you that we at *Kentucky Monthly* are looking forward to the stories yet to come.

Stephen M. Vest
Editor and Publisher
Kentucky Monthly

The Bluegrass

A Preface

The place we call the Bluegrass is a lush, green land of farms, picturesque streams and rivers, a few cities and a lot of small towns. Its roads, some of which began as buffalo trails or even "warriors'" paths, are shaded by towering hardwood trees, and its people are friendly and hospitable, as they have been since many of their ancestors arrived in Kentucky more than two centuries ago.

There also is a timeless quality to the Bluegrass, something in the atmosphere that speaks of memory and tradition. It has always been this way.

Daniel Boone, upon seeing the region for the first time on June 7, 1769, wrote, "From the top of an eminence, we saw with pleasure the beautiful level of Kentucke. We found everywhere abundance of wild beasts of every sort, through this vast forest. The buffalo were more frequent than I have seen cattle in the settlements, browsing on the leaves of the cane, or cropping the herbage on those extensive plains."

Early English topographer Gilbert Imlay, who had explored much of the Bluegrass while trying his hand as a land speculator after the Revolutionary War, wrote in 1792 that it was "the finest and most luxuriant country, perhaps, on earth."

The Bluegrass, also known as the Outer Bluegrass, is actually a geological region of land on an arched limestone foundation encompassing about eight thousand square miles, forty present-day counties and one-fifth of the state, bounded by the sandstone Mississippian plateaus of south central Kentucky to the south, the mountainous Cumberland Escarpment to the east and the Ohio River to the north and east.

The Inner Bluegrass, the land surrounding Lexington, is made up of gently rolling hills and slowly meandering streams, separated from the

Bluegrass by a series of higher hills. It encompasses all or parts of twelve to fifteen counties, including Fayette, Woodford, Franklin, Anderson, Jessamine, Mercer, Washington, Harrison, Bourbon, Clark and Madison.

BLUEGRASS

By definition, the grass growing in the Inner and Outer Bluegrass is blue-green in color. Etymologically, it is a pasture and meadow grass with the scientific name *Poa pratensis* that actually originated in Asia, but was naturalized in America at some early date.

Bluegrass absorbs the calcium and phosphate of the limestone upon which it rests, creating a perfect pasture land for livestock of all kinds, but especially Thoroughbred horses. Phosphate, in particular, is well suited for growing tobacco, as well as alfalfa, hay and, in earlier times, hemp.

The Bluegrass contains the state's finest and most expensive agricultural land, and is one of the reasons Kentucky induced pioneers to get here in any way they could, from floating down the Ohio River to the appropriately named town of Limestone (today's Maysville), to walking for hundreds of miles through the Cumberland Gap and along the Warrior's Path or Wilderness Road.

"What a Buzzel is amongst People about Kentuck," a Virginia preacher of the time wrote. "To hear people speak of it one Would think it was a new found Paradise."

As many people who live there today will tell you, it hasn't changed a bit.

Acknowledgements

Every once in a while, someone will ask me, "Why are you always writing about history?" My usual answer is, "I have to."

It's true; I really don't have a choice. Whenever I hear a new twist on an old story or run across an old newspaper article telling about an interesting person who lived here long ago, I feel absolutely compelled to learn more about it and, in turn, tell others.

I love Kentucky and have spent at least the last thirty years reading about our state and its history. It is endlessly interesting to me and I think it would be equally interesting to any Kentuckian who could easily find the stories.

Along the way I've met many kindred spirits who also are compelled to preserve, research and interpret Kentucky history, and have made my efforts much easier in many ways. Many of them also have become good friends. Thanks to the following:

Dr. Thomas H. Appleton Jr. has been a friend and mentor ever since he helped hire me at the Kentucky Historical Society (KHS) in April 1995. He has helped in myriad ways over the years, but perhaps mostly in giving me the confidence to realize that I have an ability to interpret history in an interesting way.

Dr. Melba Porter Hay, my division manager at KHS, has helped support my efforts in good times and bad, for which I'm profoundly grateful. Chapter 16 is based on her research.

Annie Denny and the late Carol McGurk, personifications of Kentucky hospitality, have helped instill a love for the past in untold numbers of museum visitors over the years.

John Trowbridge, a born researcher. Over the last decade or so, John has found and secured the gravesites of countless Kentuckians who served in the nation's wars, from African American Union soldiers whose graves were being compromised by a road-widening project to War of 1812 veterans' graves mistakenly paved over at the State Mound Memorial in Frankfort Cemetery. Chapter 8 is based on his research.

Lynn Hollingsworth, a fine archivist, often has facilitated my efforts to learn more about Kentuckians of the past.

Mike Hudson, another former KHS colleague and a good researcher, whose passion is putting together museum exhibits.

Jake Turner, who handles much of the work at KHS that museum exhibits require, and takes great pride in helping tell the stories.

And, last but not least, I'd like to thank Steve Vest, editor and publisher of *Kentucky Monthly* magazine, for allowing me a platform for more than a decade now to communicate our state's interesting stories to Kentuckians everywhere.

Thanks everyone!

Another Name for Heaven

Pristine and primeval in the mid-1700s, Kentucky first entered the consciousness of American colonists as an "Eden" or "El Dorado of the West," the next place an energetic young man could enter penniless and see his dreams come true.

Virginian Dr. Thomas Walker explored it in 1750, and explorers called "long hunters" from the Carolinas, including Daniel Boone, came scouting land in the 1760s and 1770s. This was in defiance of King George's Proclamation of 1763, which prohibited exploration and settlement west of the Appalachian Mountains.

Kentucky was a land of extreme contrasts. An explorer could be awed by its beauty and promise in one moment and in a terrifying fight for his life the next.

General Robert B. McAfee remembered:

> *In these years...* [it] *began to circulate that there was a rich and delightful country to the west on the waters of the Ohio...My father and uncles often held councils together and talked over their future prospects, all of whom being in the vigor of manhood and full of enterprise and adventure, longed to see for themselves, as they could not think of being confined to the sterile mountains of Virginia where only small parcels of fertile land could be found at any one place.*

Revolutionary Settlers

By the 1770s, explorers had given way to settlers—often Revolutionary War soldiers whose enlistments had expired—who began seeking to

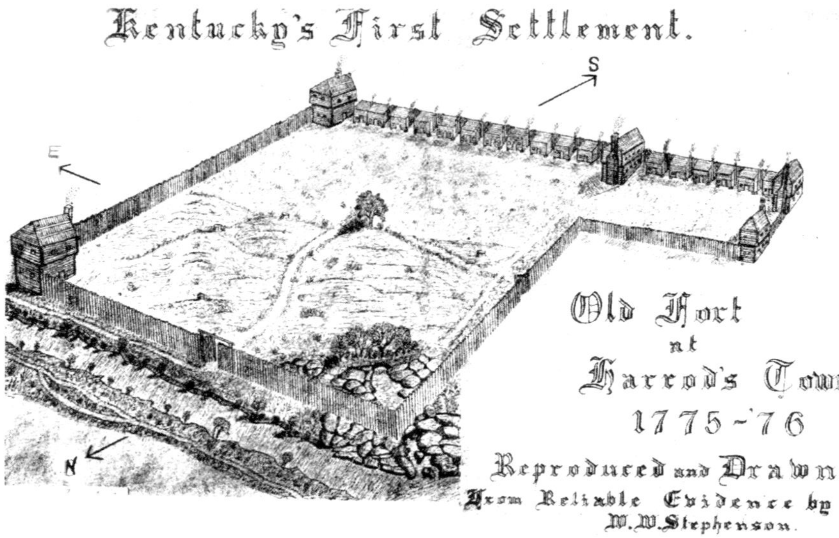

Kentucky's first settlement, Harrodsburg, began in 1774 as a row of separate cabins in the wilderness. By the next year, it was a fort. *Courtesy of* Kentucky Monthly *magazine.*

secure land for themselves and their families. Under the Virginia land law, a pioneer possessing a land warrant—often payment for military service—or other right to own land had to locate an unclaimed parcel, enter his claim and have a survey done and recorded before he acquired ownership. This proved easier said than done in the middle of a war.

Kentucky's first settlement, Harrodsburg, began in 1774 as a row of separate cabins in the wilderness. By the next year, Harrodsburg was a fort.

"STOCKADING UP"

To make settlements militarily defensible, pioneers constructed stockades to encircle them. This process began by clearing an area of trees, often either one square acre of land or an equal amount in a rectangular shape. The chopped-down trees were used for construction material. Experienced pioneers, armed only with axes, saws and augers, could convert felled trees into almost anything they needed, from long logs for the stockade and cabin to flat-sided logs for floors to slivers of split logs for clapboards and roof shingles. Pegs were whittled from smaller pieces for use in the place of nails or other fasteners.

"Stockading up," as pioneers described it, meant digging a trench three feet deep into which were placed fifteen-foot-long logs set vertically. The process was described by historian Alfred Pirtle in the 1920s: "One end of each piece was sharpened with the ax so that the pieces of timber when placed on end and so close together that there were no places for a bullet to go through, formed an edge like a saw…The earth was rammed tight around the stockade, and in a few months it was perfectly firm."

Doors were made of split logs made straight on two sides and held together with pegs. Shutters were the only way to close a window opening, which was usually also accomplished with a peg. A door would have a latch that fit into a carved depression to make it secure. A hole was generally carved into the wood above the latch, from which a string would be passed to allow the latch to be operated from the outside. In times of crisis, the string would be pulled inside. Larger holes—to accommodate rifles—also were bored for "fire-throughs."

A stockade's effectiveness was that logs would stop rifle balls, coupled with the fact that Indian attackers didn't possess artillery.

Land

The reason to come to Kentucky was to secure land. Regardless of the dangers posed by their enemies, these land-hungry pioneers weren't about to cower inside a fort while more aggressive neighbors established claims to the best land. So they left the forts in search of their future homes, well aware of the risks they were taking. The shelters they constructed often were simply fortified cabins, or cabins either within or part of an enclosed stockade.

Oftentimes pioneers traveled together in extended family groups. Their settlements sometimes became known as stations, though the terms "station" and "fort" were commonly used interchangeably. Kentucky soon had a network of stations, and it was the duty of every man who could carry a rifle to come to the aid of a station under attack. This arrangement was vital to the survival of all because Kentuckians were almost always outnumbered. It has been estimated that Boonesborough, founded by Daniel Boone, contained no more than 150 men, women and children when it was established in 1774, and the numbers at most other stations were much smaller.

The situation changed with General George Rogers Clark's successful 1778–79 military campaign to secure the frontier. With the Indian threat diminished, Kentucky was poised for its very first immigration explosion.

GETTING THERE

There were two main ways to enter Kentucky: via the Wilderness Road through the Cumberland Gap or on the Ohio River to Limestone (present-day) Maysville and the Falls of the Ohio (present-day Louisville). To walk through the gap—the largest break in the Appalachian Mountains for hundreds of miles—settlers gathered at Sycamore Shoals, in present-day Tennessee, or at other rendezvous points along the Powell, Clinch and Holston Valleys in Virginia and North Carolina, then to Martin's Station in western Virginia, southeast of the gap.

Some came with military land warrants, either earned or purchased. Others, sometimes "almost naked, paddling bare-foot and bare-legged along, or laboring up the rocky hills," arrived with nothing more tangible than the hope that their new home would be better than their old.

Residents of whole communities in the East got caught up in the excitement, sold out and began assembling at places such as Fort Pitt—present-day Pittsburgh and the beginning of the Ohio River—Fort Redstone, Pennsylvania, and the Monongahela Valley in present-day West Virginia.

Most loaded their belongings in flatboats or keelboats, the largest of which—known as Kentucky boats—could hold a minimum of ten tons of supplies, furnishings and even livestock. The more desperate often made the journey in dugout canoes. John Floyd, whose letters form much of what historians know about early Kentucky, reported in the spring of 1780 that "near 300 large boats have arrived this spring at the falls (present-day Louisville) with families."

Nicholas Meriwether wrote his father-in-law, Captain William Meriwether, on August 7, 1784, with advice about a flatboat trip to Kentucky: "Sail all night unless exceeding dark & be upon the way earley in the mornings when you do stop & stay but little time at a place. This well Obsurv'd you'll find it very trifleing to come down the river; and not the least dainger—We wish much to see you dow[n] safe; and live in hopes you'll come this fall."

In the midst of such a phenomenon, a Virginia preacher, trying to explain the eternal reward to his congregation, said, "O my dear honeys, heaven is a Kentucky of a place."

DANIEL BOONE

One newcomer was John Filson, a thirty-two-year-old schoolteacher who came to Kentucky in the autumn of 1783 to acquire land to sell to others.

It has been estimated that Boonesborough, founded by Daniel Boone, contained no more than 150 men, women and children when it was established in 1774, and the numbers at most other stations were much smaller. *Courtesy of* Kentucky Monthly *magazine.*

As a way to market his investment, Filson wrote and published a book, *The Discovery, Settlement, and Present State of Kentucke*. It included a fine map and an appendix, which Filson titled *The Adventures of Colonel Daniel Boon*.

Filson's book not only attracted settlers from the seaboard states and Europe, but it also made Daniel Boone a household name for all time.

THE FIRST IMMIGRANTS

Those attracted to the infant Kentucky were mainly English and Ulster Scots (Scottish Protestants from Northern Ireland), but also Welsh and German, many of whom brought the African American slaves they had acquired in America. At statehood—June 1, 1792—Kentucky was a literal land of opportunity populated by Revolutionary War veterans, non-inheriting sons of wealthy easterners, land-hungry poor farmers and, perhaps more importantly, their families.

Kentucky's first leaders reflected its general ethnic makeup. Isaac Shelby, elected the new state's first governor, was a grandson of a

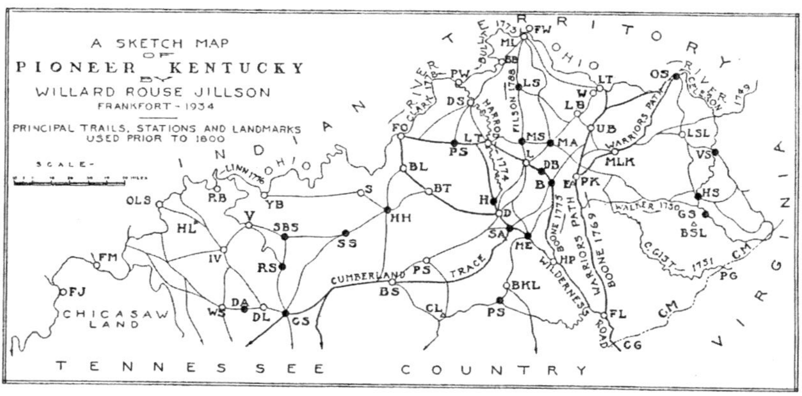

INDEX TO MAP OF PIONEER KENTUCKY.

H–Harrod's Fort; B–Boonesboro; FO–Falls of the Ohio; PS–Painted Stone Station; LT–Leestown; L–Lexington; D–Danville; SA–St. Asaph's; ME–Moore's and English's Stations; HP–Hazel Patch; FL–Flat Lick; CG–Cumberland Gap; PG–Pound Gap. HS–Harman's Station; VS–Vancouver's Station; FW–Fort Washington; LT–Limestone; W–Washington; OS–Old Shawnee Town; LB–Lower Blue Licks; UB–Upper Blue Licks; E–Eskippakithiki; MA–Martin's Station; MS–McClelland's Station; LS–Littel's Station. BB–Big Bone Lick; DB–Boone's Station; BT–Bardstown; RS–Rhode's Station; HH–Haycraft, Helm and Hyne's Station; SS–Shaw's Station; PS–Price's Settlement; DA–Davis Station; BS–Blue Spring; CS–Cook's Station; YB–Yellow Bank; RB–Red Bank; S–Big Spring; IV–Indian Village. SBS–Smither's and Barnett's Stations; OLS–Old Lower Shawnee Town; FM–Fort Massic; FJ–Fort Jefferson; OP–Ouasioto Pass; DS–Drennon Springs; BL–Bullitt's Lick; LSL–Little Sandy Licks; BSL–Boone's Salt Lick; GS–Graham's Station; V–Vienna. PS–Pittman's Station; BKL–Big Knob Lick; ML–Mouth of Licking; PW–Port William; CM–Cumberland Mountain; PK–Pilot Knob; MLK–Mud Lick; HL–Highland Lick; DL–Double Lick; CL–Cumberland Lick; WS–Woods' Settlement.

Pioneers devised a sound system of defense using stockades—often called either stations or forts—which protected them in times of attack. If one station or fort was attacked, settlers from others nearby would come to its defense. Stations were also used as bases, in which a pioneer's family would stay while he was out hunting land for permanent settlement.

Welshman; Attorney General George Nicholas is believed to have been a descendant of a British navy surgeon; Speaker of the Senate Alexander Scott Bullitt's family was French; while House Speaker Robert Breckinridge was a descendant of an Ulster Scot family.

It was an energetic population of rugged individualists, anxious to build a prosperous future in their new home. They cleared the land for farms, fought and helped win another war with Great Britain and built the beginnings of the state's cities.

Ulster Scots

Scottish colonists of Northern Ireland—the Ulster Scots—began streaming into America as early as 1632. By the time of the Revolution, more than a half million of them had emigrated, accounting for about one sixth of the entire American population. Frontier Kentucky received the Ulster Scots from virtually every coastal settlement, but especially from the Carolinas. As was usually the case, these veteran colonists headed straight for the frontier, bearing the brunt of the hardships of pioneering, but also securing a large share of the opportunities. Such quintessentially Kentucky names as Breckinridge, Todd, Logan, McAfee and McCracken all have Ulster Scot origins.

It was John Finley—son of an Ulster Scot emigrant to Pennsylvania—who guided Daniel Boone into Kentucky in 1769 and James Henry Knox, of a County Antrim family, who helped explore it.

Slaves and Religious Refugees

African American slaves came to Kentucky with their white "owners." As early as 1761, Christopher Gist explored land along the Ohio River with his black "servant." In 1773, it was a slave named Adam who accompanied Daniel Boone's son James in a quest for supplies and returned to tell Boone of his son's torture and murder.

Some newcomers saw Kentucky as an opportunity to enjoy religious freedom. Exiled for their faith, French Catholics nurtured the Catholic beginnings not only of Kentucky, but of the entire Midwest, and founded a religious order at Loretto, in Nelson County. Meanwhile, French Protestants, known as Huguenots, arrived in the 1780s to help found the Traveling Church, which helped establish Baptists in the state.

In part because of that nation's indispensible help during the Revolutionary War, the French exerted an influence on early Kentucky disproportionate to their numbers. Though representing only 1.6 percent of the state's 1790 population, French immigrants brought religion and culture—as well as democratic political theories—to the infant state.

French natives or descendants brought with them such familiar names as Hardin, Bullitt, Trabue, Flournoy, Chapeze, Shryock, Jouett, DuPont and LaRue. All found acceptance in a new land sprinkled with French names, from the cities of Versailles, Paris and LaGrange to the counties of Fayette and Bourbon.

All of these and more were attracted to this new place rich with opportunity, and many developed a deep affection for their state that seemed greater than that exhibited by the citizens of other states.

Robert Breckinridge—who went from trying murder cases as an attorney to saving souls as a Presbyterian minister—was on his way back to Fayette County in 1847 after spending a disappointing year as a college president in Pennsylvania. "Oh! Me," he said. "It is a great thing to be a Kentuckian."

The Revolution's Last Battle

Today's Bluegrass is a beautiful place of forests, lakes and streams, farms, suburbs and a few mid-sized and small cities. Its people are friendly and hospitable but struggle to better themselves in a rapidly changing world.

Rewind time a couple of centuries or so and you'd see the Bluegrass as a beautiful place of forests, lakes and streams, an almost untouched wilderness of unfathomable natural riches and potential. Its two thousand or so people were warm, loyal and hospitable, willing to come to the aid of a neighbor in need or ferociously defend themselves in an instant. All of them were risk-takers, the most audacious Americans to be found in the infant United States of America. Simply stated, they were willing to bet their lives—and in many cases those of their families—for the opportunity to own land in this place many considered a new paradise.

Risky Proposition

The opportunity was here, but so was the risk. Kentucky in 1782, for example, was the new place to be, with the Revolution winding down and land available to anyone willing to find it, survey it and record it in the land office. The British government, however, was still inciting its Indian allies living in present-day Ohio and elsewhere to attack the settlements, and Kentuckians devised a system to deal with the threat.

Settlers went about their business of locating, clearing and inhabiting land, tending livestock, planting crops and building cabins. In the event of attack, they "forted up" in stockades or "stations" until help could arrive from other stations nearby. It was a good system that ensured survival in perilous times. But the pioneers' enemies knew their strategy well and decided to take advantage of it. British commanders in Detroit organized Canadian soldiers and American Tories loyal to the Crown to manage larger groups of Indians and guide them in raids on Kentucky.

Only about 1,000 men in all of Kentucky were able to shoulder arms. And they were widely distributed, with about 150 in Fayette County, 500 in Lincoln County and about 350 in Jefferson County.

CALDWELL'S RAID ON BRYAN STATION

Lord Cornwallis had surrendered to General George Washington at Yorktown, Virginia, the previous October, effectively ending the American Revolution. Undeterred by this development, a force of about 1,250 Canadians, American Tories and Indians crossed the Ohio River in August 1782 and headed south along the old buffalo road toward Lexington. They consisted of 50 Canadian troops (known as Butler's Rangers) and their Tory allies commanded by Captain William Caldwell and about 300 Shawnee, Delaware, Mingo, Wyandot, Miami, Ottawa, Ojibwa and Pottawatomi Indians led by Alexander McKee, Simon Girty and Matthew Elliott. Girty was the feared Indian leader who had begun his boyhood as a white Indian captive.

Feigning attacks on other stations to attract frontiersmen away from their target, the British and Indians arrived at Bryan Station on the morning of August 16 and hid in the woods to await a chance to attack. They didn't know it, but they had been found out by settler William Tomlinson Sr., who arrived in time to forewarn the station's defenders.

Plan B called for the attackers to take advantage of the Kentuckians' habit of converging on the threatened side of a fort, abandoning the other three sides. A small force, accordingly, pretended an attack with musket fire, while the main force hid in the woods near the station's opposite side and waited for the settlers to leave their posts. The Kentuckians didn't budge.

WATER

Bryan Station was extremely vulnerable in one regard: it wasn't built around a water source. The site was, instead, chosen for its strategic hillside command of the area; the spring fifty or so yards along the Elkhorn Creek bottomland below was considered close enough to provide for the needs of the station's inhabitants.

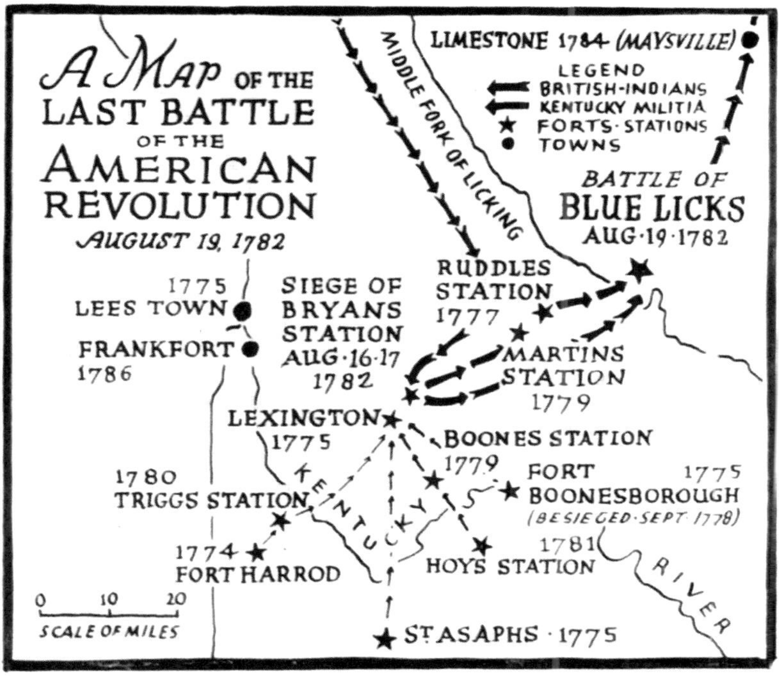

This map of the Battle of the Blue Licks was part of a painting by George Gray for the Works Progress Administration of the 1930s. Fought on August 19, 1782, it is almost universally considered the last battle of the American Revolution. *Courtesy of the Kentucky Historical Society.*

Someone inside the fort proposed that if the station's women simply walked out of the gate the following morning to obtain water from the spring—as they normally did—the Indians waiting to ambush the men probably wouldn't show themselves. It was a gamble, but without water the station would fall anyway.

What happened next is a mixture of documented pioneer accounts and legend. After at first nearly rejecting the idea, the women of the station agreed to try the plan. As the sun rose the next morning, twelve women and sixteen of their daughters—said to have been led by Jemima Suggett Johnson—emerged from Bryan Station carrying their empty vessels and headed downhill toward the spring as if nothing had happened. Knowing any slipup would result in instant death, they calmly filled the containers—a process that took as much as an hour or so—and slowly made their way back to the protection of the stockade.

The attackers made a few more attempts to lure the men out and then tried attacking with rifle fire and flaming arrows, but the station held. Rumors were flying that Kentucky militiamen were on their way, and the British and Indians decided to end their siege on August 17—not, however, before torching any crops and cabins they could find and slaughtering the settlers' livestock.

PURSUIT

The alarm had indeed been sounded, and 182 men under Colonel John Todd and Lieutenant Colonels Stephen Trigg and Daniel Boone arrived the following day. An officers' council of war was held to decide whether the militiamen should go off in hot pursuit of the enemy or await the arrival of Benjamin Logan, commander of the Lincoln County militia. When Major Hugh McGary suggested waiting, Todd accused him of "timidity." It was decided that the force should not wait for Logan, but try to overtake their retreating foes, and they followed their trail forty miles before stopping for the night.

BLUE LICKS

The next morning, August 19, the Kentuckians reached the Licking River and could plainly see Indians observing them. Todd called another council and asked Boone his opinion. The enemy was attempting an ambush, Boone said, explaining that he saw that they were concealing their numbers by walking in each other's footprints and making their trail easy to follow. He even knew where the ambush would happen: in a series of ravines near a spring and salt lick known as the Blue Licks.

After looking at their previous night's campsite, Boone estimated the enemy's strength at about five hundred. The Kentuckians were outnumbered nearly three to one. When Boone told Todd that "it is not prudent to pursue," it was more than McGary could stand. Stung by Todd's earlier questioning of his courage, he leaped upon his horse and headed it into the direction of the Indians. "Them that ain't cowards," McGary yelled, "follow me."

The men dutifully obeyed, thinking the officers' decision had been made. They formed into their previously determined divisions and marched toward Blue Licks. The officers could only scramble after them.

It was too late to stop. "We are all slaughtered men," said Boone, waiting for the ambush to begin.

Todd and McGary's divisions were in the center of the Kentuckians' line of battle, with Major Silas Harlan's men in the front, while Trigg and Boone took the right and left, respectively. The moment Harlan's twenty-five men crested a hill overlooking the ravines, the British and Indians opened fire. The Kentuckians' center ceased to exist and the right staggered. Only Boone's fifty men moved forward into the onslaught. Todd and Trigg fell from their horses dead and their men turned and fled back down the hill, many trying to free themselves from Indians as they ran.

Panic

McGary galloped up to Boone and told him that all was lost. Boone attempted to lead his men in an orderly withdrawal. Grabbing a riderless horse, he yelled to his son Israel to mount and get away. The son refused to leave his father's side, however, and was shot through the neck. He quickly died. Sergeant Aaron Reynolds, on horseback and assured of getting away, spotted Captain Robert Patterson struggling to run. Knowing the captain was nursing an old tomahawk wound, Reynolds turned the horse over to him.

This popular lithograph from the 1879 book *Sketches of Western Adventure*, by John A. McClung, shows Aaron Reynolds heroically giving up his horse to a wounded Captain Robert Patterson during the routed settlers' frantic retreat from the Blue Licks battle.

The ford of the one-hundred-foot-wide Licking River was narrow, and the frantic men couldn't find it quickly. "Some of the fugitives were overtaken on the way to the river and fell beneath the stroke of Indiana hatchet and spear," wrote historian Humphrey Marshall a few years after the battle. "Some were slain in the water, some on either shore."

By the time Logan and his 150-strong Lincoln County militia arrived, it was all over. Logan's men helped the wounded back to their stations and, with some of the survivors, went back to Blue Licks on August 24 to bury the dead. "We…found their bodies scattered everywhere, cut and mangled in a dreadful manner," Boone wrote. Reynolds made his way back to Bryan Station, where a thankful Patterson gave him two hundred acres of land for saving his life.

AFTERMATH

"So valiantly did our small party fight, to the memory of those who unfortunately fell in the Battle, enough of Honour cannot be paid,"

John Filson's 1783 book *The Discovery, Settlement, and Present State of Kentucke* immortalized Daniel Boone for all time, but distorted his true nature and formidable frontier abilities. The real Boone preferred a brimmed beaver hat to a coonskin cap, and wasn't sure if he was responsible for the death of even one Indian. *Lithograph by H. Schile, 1874. Courtesy of the Library of Congress.*

Boone wrote in a letter to Virginia Governor Benjamin Harrison. He also appealed for military help. "I have encouraged the people in this country all that I could, but I can no longer justify them or myself to risk our lives here under such extraordinary hazards," Boone wrote. "The inhabitants of this country are very much alarmed at the thoughts of the Indians bringing another campaign into our country this Fall. If this should be the case, it will break up these settlements."

The federal militia commander in Kentucky, General George Rogers Clark, organized an expedition against the Ohio Indian villages in November 1782. More than one thousand men participated, including Benjamin Logan and Daniel Boone. When the Shawnee retreated north, the Kentuckians burned five villages, crops and stores of food along the Great Miami River and returned home.

In 1786, a force under Logan attacked the northern villages along the Mad River and destroyed them. Hugh McGary walked up to Moluntha, a captured Shawnee chief, and asked him if he had been at Blue Licks. Moluntha, who didn't understand the question, nodded in assent anyway. An enraged McGary pulled out his tomahawk and buried it into the chief's skull. He was relieved of his command and later court-martialed.

These expeditions reduced the Indian threat to Kentucky by the time it entered the Union in 1792. When the state legislature began creating new counties, members named six of them Todd, Harlan, Trigg, Logan, Clark and Boone.

Senior Statesman

We all have those times in our lives when we have a decision to make, a momentous choice between paths that might lead to great success or great failure. John Brown Jr. faced such a decision early in life. It was autumn 1776, and the American Revolution was raging, with the British army—largest, best-equipped and most feared in the world—chasing a ragtag group of fleeing American rebels under a seemingly inept commander named George Washington.

The youthful Brown had grown up comfortably in Staunton, Virginia, where his father, John Sr., was a respected Presbyterian minister and educator. His mother was the former Margaret Preston. The family finances allowing him to pursue the education of a gentleman, Brown excelled at his father's school—known as Liberty Hall Academy—before moving on to the College of New Jersey, which would later take on the name of its location, Princeton.

From Student to Militiaman

With the college in chaos and the British army approaching the town, Brown made his decision: he would join the retreating American militiamen in their fight. Serving as a volunteer, the nineteen-year-old crossed the Delaware River with Washington's troops and earned respect enough to later serve as an aide to General Lafayette.

By 1778, he was back in Virginia, enrolling at the College of William and Mary. Abandoning his initial thoughts of becoming a doctor, the young man pursued a career in law. As capital of the colony of Virginia,

Williamsburg was perhaps the finest place in America to study law, and Brown learned from the best: Edmund Randolph, George Wythe and Thomas Jefferson. Again excelling in his studies, he became one of the first members of the Phi Beta Kappa academic honor fraternity.

CONTINENTAL CONGRESSMAN

Soon after studying with Jefferson, Brown became a lawyer and almost immediately moved to Danville, in Virginia's District of Kentucky, in the summer of 1783. His credentials made him, at twenty-six, immediately respected, and he was chosen to represent the district in the Virginia Senate for the next five years, before becoming a member of the Continental Congress (1787–88).

Having served during the Revolution and as a member of the Continental Congress, Brown knew George Washington, James Madison, John Adams and James Monroe, in addition to Jefferson. These associations and friendships with the founding fathers gave him enormous influence, allowing him opportunities to shape political events to Kentucky's benefit.

Upon ratification of the U.S. Constitution, Brown served in the U.S. House from 1789 to 1792, representing Kentucky's interests as it pursued a separation from Virginia. But there remained work to be done. In 1791, with Kentucky still attempting to defend itself against Indian attacks, Congress appointed him, along with General—later governor—Charles Scott, Benjamin Logan, Harry Innes and Isaac Shelby, as a Board of War for the Kentucky District. The men were given the power to defend the settlements and Brown helped organize several expeditions, and even joined one as a private under the command of his brother James.

Brown negotiated with Spain to secure for Kentuckians the right to navigate the Mississippi River, opening a vital market for their products in New Orleans.

Like Henry Clay after him, Brown's legal abilities allowed him to quickly grow wealthy helping clients settle disputes arising from Kentucky's hopelessly tangled land system.

U.S. Senator from Kentucky

When the state was officially established on June 1, 1792, Brown was elected one of its first two U.S. senators. Once it was decided that Frankfort would be the permanent capital, he moved there and began building a home on a four-acre town lot he purchased along the Kentucky River. He decided to call it Liberty Hall, after his father's academy.

The home would be built in the Federal style Brown had known in Virginia, perhaps influenced by Jefferson's architectural inclinations. He cleared land and workmen dug a basement, the clay from which was used to make bricks for the house.

In his travels, Brown had become acquainted with a young woman named Margaretta Brown, a minister's daughter from New York City.

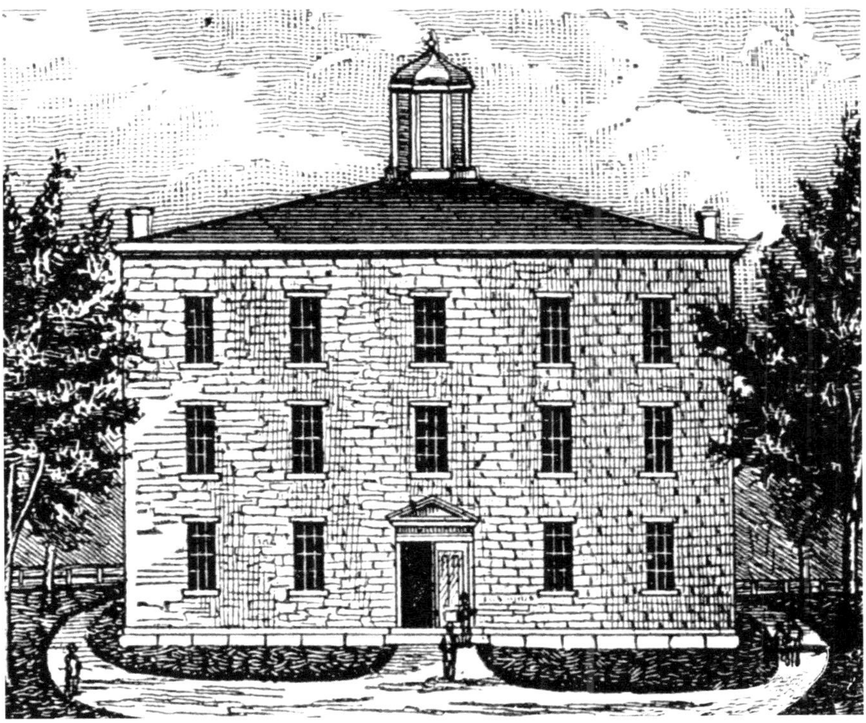

Frankfort's first State Capitol Building was erected in 1794 and destroyed by fire in 1813. For a year after Kentucky gained statehood in 1792, Lexington served as the home of the state government, and the capitol building was a log cabin located between Mill and Broadway Streets.

He married her on February 21, 1799, and brought her to Frankfort to preside over his newly finished home in the spring of 1801.

The couple already had an infant son, Mason, when they arrived in Frankfort, and over the next few years, four more children—Orlando, Alfred, Alfred II and Euphemia Helm—would add their voices to Liberty Hall. Brown built a smokehouse, carriage house, stables and slave quarters. A formal garden was placed in the backyard and stairs were built into the hillside, leading to a boat landing on the river.

But Brown was still a U.S. senator, and was often in Washington. In the 1800 presidential election, when Thomas Jefferson and Aaron Burr had an equal number of electoral votes and the contest was to be decided by the House of Representatives, Brown lobbied tirelessly for his friend Thomas Jefferson, who won. The new president, in turn, offered his former pupil numerous federal appointments, all of which he turned down to remain in the Senate. Brown served as Senate president pro tempore in 1804–05 (which today would make him third in line for the presidency). His term ended, Brown went home to Liberty Hall and declined public office—including presidential appointments—for the rest of his life.

RETIREMENT

Brown's home became a place of parties, balls and formal dinners, a pleasant retreat from a career of public service. Sadly, only two of John and Margaretta's children survived to adulthood. Mason, the eldest, was a graduate of Yale, a prominent attorney and circuit court judge. He also served as Kentucky's secretary of state and was one of the founders of the Frankfort Cemetery. His son, Benjamin Gratz Brown, would become a U.S. senator and governor of Missouri. Orlando was a Princeton graduate and attorney who served as U.S. commissioner of Indian affairs under President Zachary Taylor.

As he entered his seventies, John Brown began to worry about the inheritance he would leave his two sons. Anxious to divide things absolutely equally, he decided to divide his land into two lots, leaving the Liberty Hall portion to Mason. On the vacant portion, he would build a house for Orlando, commissioning celebrated Kentucky architect Gideon Shryock to do the job. The house was completed in 1835 for the then-princely sum of $5,000.

The Browns' Liberty Hall was home to U.S. senators, a vice presidential candidate, a governor of Missouri, a U.S. commissioner of the Bureau of Indian Affairs, an ambassador to France, a U.S. district attorney and three U.S. Army colonels. John Brown's service to Kentucky included his enormous influence in national politics. Over his career, he established the nation's "first western state" on equal footing with the original thirteen, helped secure its safety and opened the New Orleans market to its citizens. *Photo by Theodore Webb. Courtesy of the Library of Congress.*

When Orlando—by this time a local attorney and editor of the *Frankfort Commonwealth* newspaper—wanted to establish an institution to preserve Kentucky's history, John Brown was happy to help. He presided over a meeting held in the present Old State Capitol on April 22, 1836, to establish the Kentucky Historical Society.

When Brown died the following year, on August 28, 1837, he held the distinction of being the last surviving member of the Continental Congress. Margaretta followed him on May 28, 1838, and both were buried in Frankfort Cemetery.

But Liberty Hall and the Orlando Brown House were to live on. Louisville attorney John Matthew Scott, a great-grandson of the Browns, sold the property to Liberty Hall Inc.—which had been formed by preservation-minded citizens of Frankfort—and it opened as a museum in 1937. Anne Hord Brown, the Browns' last surviving great-grandchild, deeded the Orlando Brown House to the National Society of the Colonial Dames of America in 1955. Today the entire property is operated as Liberty Hall Historic Site.

Shelby

Shelby. Today it's a name for dogs and little girls, but in early Kentucky, it was almost the same as saying "Washington."

Isaac Shelby was born on December 11, 1750, just west of Hagerstown, Maryland, the grandson of Welsh immigrants. As a boy and young man, through experience and observation, he absorbed the business of his father until, by his early adulthood, he was an accepted expert. The family business was warfare.

From 1755 to 1781, men on the American frontier were in almost a constant struggle with the French, British or Indians and sometimes whole families were wiped out because they dared to live west of accepted settlements. But the Shelbys were well suited for the cards that fate dealt them. Isaac was described as possessing "indefatigable perseverance" and, like his father, "born with a strong constitution, capable of bearing great privation and fatigue."

Evan Shelby had been a fur trader and owner of twenty-four thousand acres in Maryland—in addition to being a frontier military leader—before losses associated with Indian struggles forced the family to move to the Holston Valley in what is now East Tennessee. The elder Shelby soon successfully built a thriving farm on the present-day site of Bristol, Tennessee, and became the highest-ranking militia officer on the Southern frontier, with the rank of brigadier general.

By the time he was twenty-one, Isaac had been a surveyor, sheriff of Fredericktown, Virginia, and a veteran of his father's various military expeditions. At the end of the daylong Battle of Point Pleasant on October 10, 1774, Evan Shelby was the highest ranking officer to survive the fighting, and Isaac, serving as a lieutenant, led the flanking maneuver into the Indian rear that secured colonial victory.

Isaac Shelby, born on December 11, 1750, in Maryland, had a virtual lifetime of military experience behind him by the time he took office as Kentucky first governor in 1792. Serving another term when the War of 1812 broke out, he took command of Kentucky's units himself and helped win the Battle of the Thames that helped end the war on terms favorable to the United States. He also helped establish Kentucky's southwestern border and suggested the design of the state seal and its motto. He died on July 18, 1826. *Courtesy of the Kentucky Historical Society.*

The youthful Shelby traveled to Kentucky in 1775 to survey lands for himself and others. During the Revolutionary War, he helped supply the Continental army and provided boats for General George Rogers Clark's Illinois campaign that won the Northwest Territory for the United States.

After serving in the Virginia legislature in 1779 and helping to establish the western boundary with North Carolina, Shelby learned that he was actually a citizen of the latter colony. The following year, at age thirty, he was appointed colonel of the Sullivan County, North Carolina militia, and later served in the new state's legislature.

Upon hearing the disastrous news of the American defeat in South Carolina and the surrender of Charles Town in May 1780—which cast deep shadows on the Patriot cause—Shelby brought his Sullivan County militiamen to meet with John Sevier and other frontier leaders about confronting the army of British regulars.

Pushing the Envelope

The redcoats were considered the finest fighting men the world, and American militia had never defeated them. Assembling a force under various frontier commanders, all providing their own weapons and supplies and acting on their own initiative, the 910 men found British Major Patrick Ferguson at Kings Mountain in northern South Carolina.

Ferguson, dug in and outnumbering the Americans two to one, declared that "God Almighty could not drive me (out)." With Shelby commanding the middle of three columns, the Americans attacked the mountain and—in less than an hour—surrounded and killed Ferguson and 375 of his officers and men, capturing 730. American casualties numbered 28 killed and 60 wounded.

The Battle of Kings Mountain forced some of the moves by British Lieutenant General Charles Cornwallis that resulted in Washington's victory at Yorktown, Virginia, which gained America its independence. North Carolina presented its hero with a handsome sword in honor of the victory. But Kentucky beckoned.

Kentucky

Shelby arrived at Boonesborough in 1783 and in May of that year married Captain Nathaniel Hart's daughter, Susanna. Shelby settled on the land he had surveyed in 1775—the first preemption granted in Kentucky—and began construction of its first stone house, a two-story home five miles south of Danville. He called it Traveler's Rest.

Shelby served as a member of the Danville conventions that led to statehood for Kentucky, and, in April 1792 was a member of its first constitutional convention, also held in Danville. The following month, under the just-written rules, a group of electors met in the temporary capital in Lexington and chose Isaac Shelby to be Kentucky's first governor. On inauguration day, June 4—the third day of the commonwealth's existence—Shelby rode on horseback to Lexington amid drumbeats, musket and cannon fire, church bells and the applause of citizens who lined both sides of the road to greet him.

Shelby's term in office was filled with organizing state government, building a militia capable of securing the frontier from Indian attacks and paying for the building of roads. As state officials were attempting to establish the new state's procedures and practices, Shelby suggested the design for its seal, which was adopted on December 20, 1792. He was fond of "The Liberty Song," written by John Dickinson in 1768. The song's chorus includes the words: "They join in hand, brave Americans all; By uniting we stand, by dividing we fall." The new seal would incorporate the song's words as the state motto and include two "brave Americans" joining hands. The seal was subsequently incorporated into the design of the state's first official flag, in 1918.

WAR GOVERNOR

When the four years of his term expired, the governor set down his pen, rode back to Traveler's Rest and resumed his favorite pursuits: farming and raising cattle.

Twenty years later—as the nation moved toward another war with Great Britain—the sixty-three-year-old Shelby was urged to run again for governor, mainly to prepare the state for the beginning of hostilities. He won.

After the January 1813 military disaster at the River Raisin, in which wounded Kentucky prisoners were massacred by their Indian captors, Shelby received word from General William Henry Harrison that more troops were needed for the war effort. The governor called for two thousand volunteers to meet him at Newport in August, promising "a fair opportunity of avenging the blood of your butchered friends." Four

Shelby settled on the land he had surveyed in 1775—the first preemption granted in Kentucky—and began construction of its first stone house, a two-story home five miles south of Danville. He called it Traveler's Rest. The home was destroyed by a fire in 1905, but the family cemetery near the site is a state shrine.

thousand men turned out. Shelby took command of them and headed north. The subsequent Battle of the Thames, in modern-day Canada, was a decisive defeat for the British and helped end the war on favorable terms for the Americans.

To honor their efforts, Shelby and Harrison were awarded special gold medals by Congress. Politicians hailed the governor as "a patriot without reproach and a soldier without ambition."

A Purchase and a Reminiscence

In 1817, President James Monroe appointed the once again retired Shelby secretary of war, but he declined the appointment. He did join Andrew Jackson the following year in negotiations with the Chickasaw Indians, which led to a treaty that brought 4,600 square miles of what came to be known as the Jackson Purchase within Kentucky's borders.

The area comprises the present counties of Ballard, Calloway, Carlisle, Fulton, Graves, Hickman, Marshall and McCracken.

Looking back on his war-filled career, Shelby very aptly described himself and his men, especially those who had served at Kings Mountain.

> *These Mountaineers were poor men who lived by Keeping stock in the range beyond the Mountains. They were Volunteers and neither expected nor received any compensation except liquidated Certificates worth 2 pence in the pound…For myself for the whole services of 1780 & 1781 both in Camp and in the assembly I received a liquidated certificate…after my removal to Kentucky sold for 6 yds of Middling Broadcloth and I gave one Coat of it to the person who brought it out to me Indeed I was proud of receiving that.*

Shelby died at Traveler's Rest on July 18, 1826, at age seventy-five. He was buried nearby, beneath a monument placed by the commonwealth. Susanna Shelby died at their home on June 23, 1833.

In tribute to his leadership, nine states—Kentucky, Tennessee, Alabama, Texas, Ohio, Indiana, Illinois, Missouri and Iowa—named counties after Isaac Shelby.

Traveler's Rest was destroyed by a fire in 1905. The family cemetery, at 6725 State Route 300 just south of Danville, is a state shrine.

> *Congressional Medal Citation*
> *April 6, 1818*
> *U. States of America in Congress assembled that the thanks of Congress be and they are hereby presented to Major General W. Henry Harrison, and Isaac Shelby, late Governor of Kentucky and through them to the officers and men under their command for their gallantry and good conduct in defeating the combined British and Indian forces under Major Genl. Procter, on the Thames in upper Canada, on the 5th day of October 1813—Capturing the British army, with their baggage, camp equipage & artillery; and that the President of the United States be requested to cause two gold medals to be struck, emblematical of this triumph and presented to Genl. Harrison & Isaac Shelby late Governor of Kentucky.*
> *(Signed) H. Clay, Spk.*
> *H.R. Gaillard Pres. S. pro tem*
> *Approved James Munroe*

Lexington

One night in early June 1775, some Pennsylvania frontiersmen were sitting around a campfire along a fork of Elkhorn Creek in the Kentucky wilderness preparing their supper and getting ready to bed down for the night. As the story goes, the attention of the men turned to their campsite, the land about which they had concluded would make a good place for their future homes.

News that the long-anticipated Revolution had begun two months before had filled the men with patriotic fervor, along with righteous hatred of the British attackers of their countrymen in Massachusetts. After a few suggestions for a name for this new land had been made and rejected, there came the shout of the town in which the April battle had taken place: "Lexington."

"It was unanimously resolved," according to an early account in the *Kentucky Reporter* newspaper, "to perpetuate the first opposition by arms to British tyranny, by erecting in the then wilderness, a monument more durable than the pyramids of Egypt to the memory of these citizens murdered…And also to perpetuate their own devotion to the sacred principles of Liberty."

The men—William McConnell, James Dunkin, Isaac Greer, John McCrackin, Levi Todd, Hugh Shannon, John Maxwell and John Morrison—built a cabin that would allow them to claim the land and planted corn and snap beans before Indians drove them back to their Harrodsburg settlement.

The Revolution, however, came to Kentucky, and it would be four years before the vicinity of the campfire was safe enough for the pioneers' dream of settling it to begin. Robert Patterson, a McConnell associate, led a group

Pioneer stockades like Fort Lexington were built by placing fifteen-foot-long sharpened logs in three-foot trenches to form twelve-foot walls capable of withstanding any frontier-era attack except cannon fire.

of twenty-five frontiersmen back to the site in 1779, and the men built a blockhouse, which they promptly christened Fort Lexington, and cabins.

The first woman to arrive at the fort was John Morrison's wife, who gave birth to John Morrison Jr., the first white child born in Lexington.

As the town was surveyed and streets laid out, a newcomer—with apparent experience in such things—built a windmill somewhat near the strategic hill on which the blockhouse had been built. The road to the mill predictably acquired the name Mill Street, which it would retain ever afterward. Other points of interest eventually would conform to nondescript addresses on Lexington city streets. The site of the fort was at the intersection of Main and Mill Streets, which would later carry the address 326 West Main Street.

On the southwest corner of the intersection, John Carty built a house and began manufacturing earthenware. General James Wilkinson opened a dry goods store at 581 West Main Street. Robert Patterson, who had founded both Lexington and Cincinnati, lived at 331 Patterson Street beginning in 1783.

The first Lexington church, Mount Zion, was built by Presbyterians out of logs in 1784 at the southeastern corner of Walnut and Short Streets. The original Catholic church, also a log structure, was built in 1794 at the northeast corner of Patterson and Main Streets.

CHANGES AND IMPROVEMENTS

Lexington got its first tavern in 1785 when James Bray opened his establishment on Main near Spring Street. Before long, other taverns sprung up, such as Ayres's Cross Keys tavern at Spring and Main, the Indian Queen at High and Broadway and something called the Fried-Meat tavern. These taverns were not simply what would later be called saloons, but were also hostelries, primitive hotels in which travelers could eat and sleep and also find accommodations for their horses.

As was often the case, Broadway was originally indentified on maps as the principal cross street of Main Street, or Main Cross Street. It opened in 1785, and town trustees instituted a rule that citizens had to remove their cow and hog pens from the right of way. They also were banned from fishing from Lexington's first bridge, built over the Town Fork of the Elkhorn at Broadway and Water Street. In 1805, an ordinance was passed banning the practice of keeping panthers as pets.

John McKinney, who began teaching a school inside the fort in 1780, built a schoolhouse—the first in Kentucky—on the public square three years later.

Early Rivalry

By 1782, Lexington had grown enough for its citizens to successfully petition the Virginia General Assembly for town status, which was granted on May 6 of that year. The region's principal town, however, was Danville, founded the same year by settler John Crow. Virginia had established the new Kentucky District Court there, and—because it boasted a commodious log courthouse—Danville attracted a series of ten conventions that led to a separation from Virginia and statehood for Kentucky. Built at the intersection of pioneer roads, however, Lexington was pulling the aura of importance its way, attracting newcomers from the seaboard states and growing at a phenomenal rate.

John Bradford—who attended the Danville conventions—was dispatched by the delegates to Philadelphia to secure a printing press to promote statehood. When he began his newspaper, the *Kentucky Gazette*, on August 11, 1787, he did so in Lexington. Transylvania University, which had been founded in Danville in 1783, moved to Lexington in 1789, and the growing town's market house—built on the site of the original fort—became the first home of the Kentucky legislature when statehood began on June 1, 1792.

As historian John D. Wright has noted, "Between 1790 and 1800 the town was transformed from a rude frontier post into an attractive community of fine homes, landed estates, and diverse manufacturing and mercantile enterprises."

NEW VIRGINIA

Aspiring families like the Breckinridges and Todds assumed leadership roles in the community and it began to take on a Virginia atmosphere, from its architecture and politics to its traditions and pastimes. "They are nearly all Virginians," wrote early French travel writer Francois A. Michaux, noting a "passion for gaming and spirituous liquors."

"Horses and lawsuits comprise the usual topic of their conversation," Michaux continued. "If a traveler happens to pass by, his horse is appreciated, if he stops he is presented with a glass of whiskey."

Prominent citizens were determined to transplant the best of what they had known in the East and Europe to this new place. A library was founded in 1795, along with numerous schools and academies. The people were ravenous for culture, whether it came in the form of china or linen, the latest books or a new theater. When Dr. Samuel Brown, new head of Transylvania University's medical department, began offering to infect people with "cow-pox" as a preventative measure—a practice unheard of in the East—Lexingtonians lined up to receive his vaccinations.

WATER

One interesting fact of those early days was Lexington's water source, the Town Fork of Elkhorn Creek. Its considerable flow was more than ample for Lexington's needs. Mill races were constructed along its banks, the power of which provided the impetus for the town's early industries, including a paper mill and a lead factory.

William West arrived from Baltimore in 1788 to begin painting images of the frontier. West's brother Edward, something of a tinkerer, built a small steam engine, which he installed in a boat and tried out on a dammed up portion of Town Fork near Patterson Street. When he died in 1827, he was buried in his own garden. The stream also was known to spill its banks on rainy days, sometimes with near disastrous results.

Longtime resident Samuel D. McCullough had a childhood memory of being stranded at the schoolhouse by the rising waters of Town Fork and being tied to the pommel of a horse's saddle as his rescuer led his horse through the waters while pulling McCullough's horse.

McCullough recalled,

> *I wondered at his carefulness, but when we got to Limestone Street, corner of Main, I soon saw good reasons for his anxiety. There was a mass rushing, roaring, booming waters coming down…All Water street, with few houses upon it was a mass of seething, rushing waters. My friend urged on his horse until we came where the water covered his horse's back. It was a terrible conflict for the swimming horse against the tide. As soon as his hoofs struck the ascending ground out of the strong current, I heard my preserver* [say] *"Thank God."*

A strip of land between Water and Vine Streets was reserved for runoff until, in later times, the digging of wells on nearby farms was blamed for reducing the stream to a trickle, leaving Lexington perpetually in search of a dependable source of water.

Whipping Post

From the late 1700s up to the early 1800s, lawbreakers might face the punishment of the whipping post, which stood on Courthouse Square, just east of the corner of Main Street. The penalty for petit larceny, for example, was imprisonment in the town jail for a time and thirty-nine "stripes," or lashes, at the post. When townsfolk objected to the practice as barbaric, the jailer responded by inflicting his punishments inside the jail walls, "where the screams of the sufferer could not be heard."

As would be clearly shown in later times, Lexington was about evenly divided between those in favor of slavery and those against it. There were slave markets and slave pens in town, and two slave jails, one at 203–205 East Main Street, encompassed by high walls "crowned with iron spikes."

Fourth of July

The Fourth of July was a holiday in Lexington. The day was, in fact, so important that townspeople generally didn't work on July 3 just to get ready for the celebration.

Festivities in the early 1800s—when the town boasted about fifteen thousand inhabitants—began with a parade on Main Street. It would begin at Broadway, then known as Main Cross Street, with Lexington's brilliantly uniformed Old Infantry, founded in 1789, marching in military precision.

Next came a company of rifle sharpshooters in blue hunting shirts and coonskin and opossum-skin hats. Citizens then marched in double file, husbands and wives arm in arm. Then came the Freemasons, who wore blue and red sashes and lambskin aprons. The highlight was the Revolutionary War veterans, who brought up the rear in whatever way they could: on horseback, marching with their wives or riding in carriages or wagons.

A drum and fife corps conducted the parade to the Phoenix Hotel, and then to Limestone (later Mulberry Street) before turning southwest to Maxwell Springs' "lovely grove of native forest trees…and watered by three springs or fountains."

Paraders were then dismissed to listen to orations on Washington and the nation's founding. Sometimes the Declaration of Independence would be read, to the cheers of the crowd. Afterward, drummers "beat the call to dinner," and "heads uncovered reverently" for the prayer of thanksgiving. Then, a hearty picnic—which the ladies had prepared the previous day—began. Ladies took their places at a table of honor and were waited upon by the Freemasons and their servants. The tables were filled with bread, bacon, hams, lambs, beef and venison "all whole," along with "sweetmeats and comfits." The festivities concluded and everyone full, the "fragments," as they were called, were gathered and given to the poor.

HENRY CLAY

A brilliant twenty-year-old attorney named Henry Clay arrived in Lexington in November 1797, fresh from passing the bar in his native Virginia. Before long, the young man had begun to get rich litigating land disputes from a little office at 183 North Mill Street. He married Lucretia Hart, daughter of a local merchant, two years after his arrival in town, and by 1803 had won his first elective office, a seat in the state legislature.

Clay purchased a mansion befitting his status in 1805, which he named Ashland. He raised Thoroughbred horses and eleven children there in a busy career that took him to the pinnacle of national politics, from U.S. Speaker of the House to secretary of state to an unsuccessful quest for the presidency.

TRANSYLVANIA

When Transylvania Seminary moved from Danville to Lexington in 1789, the first classes were held in a log cabin and later in the home of

Ashland, the estate of "The Great Compromiser" Henry Clay, in Lexington. *Courtesy of the author.*

Transylvania University, founded in Danville in 1780, moved to Lexington in 1789. Beginning with the 1818–25 leadership of Horace Holley, the school experienced a golden age when it educated the nation's best and brightest, including future U.S. senators, Supreme Court justices and numerous governors. *Courtesy of the Library of Congress.*

the Reverend James Moore, who would become its first president. Early medical lectures were held in a warehouse on the southwest corner of Main and Mill Streets.

Presidents George Washington and John Adams and Vice President Aaron Burr were early contributors to the school and notable visitors have included President James Monroe, General Lafayette and Daniel Boone. Transylvania moved to Third Street and Broadway in the early 1790s.

The presidency of the Reverend Horace Holley, which began in 1818, transformed the school into Transylvania University, one of the premier institutions of learning in the United States. The school boasted brilliant professors—including Jesse Bledsoe, Constantine Rafinesque, Benjamin Dudley and Daniel Drake—and produced untold numbers of leaders, including governors, U.S. senators and congressmen, two vice presidents and two associate justices of the U.S. Supreme Court. Transylvania was one of the reasons Lexington became known as the "Athens of the West" and Kentucky earned the moniker "Mother of Governors."

By 1825, just fifty years after its founding, Lexington had literally gone from a pioneer campsite to one of the nation's most important places, already surrounded by horse farms and possessing a citizenry poised to play important roles in the history of the nation.

The Oath

Whenever a new Kentucky governor is sworn in, he or she says something that sounds strange to modern ears. Before becoming the state's chief magistrate, the governor-elect must swear that he has not "fought a duel with deadly weapons within this state or out of it, with a citizen of this state; nor have I sent or accepted a challenge to fight a duel with deadly weapons with a citizen not of this state; nor have I acted as a second in carrying a challenge, or aided or assisted any person thus offending, so help me God."

Kentucky's constitution, in fact, requires all office holders, judges and attorneys, and even such public officials such as police officers and firefighters, to swear the oath before assuming their duties. The fact that such a law has survived to the present-day speaks volumes about eighteenth- and nineteenth-century Kentucky—and the lengths lawmakers were willing to go to end the practice of dueling.

Code of Honor

Kentucky's dueling customs were a continuation of the traditions of Virginia, from which the state was formed in June 1792. The Southern code of chivalry was closely related to the code of honor, and few gentlemen were willing to face the public ridicule to which they would be subjected if they refused a challenge. According to the code, a man, upon perceiving an insult, could challenge his opponent through a "second," commonly a friend or associate acting in his behalf, demanding "satisfaction." The challenged man had the choice of "terms" (usually weapons and distance), and arrangements were made by the seconds for the duel.

The practice was designed as a fair way to settle disputes between "gentlemen." A man not conducting himself within the bounds of propriety risked being called to account "on the field of honor." Threatening or ridiculing someone, an insult to a man or his female relatives and even departures from common courtesy were acceptable reasons for a challenge. As a result, men were usually on their best behavior in public, calling each other "sir" and ending their letters with "I am, sir, your most obedient servant."

The problem of dueling gained national attention with the killing on July 11, 1804, of Alexander Hamilton by Vice President Aaron Burr in Weehawken, New Jersey. Burr had just lost an election for governor of New York and blamed Hamilton's remarks, published in the state's newspapers, for his defeat. Hamilton, the first secretary of the treasury and founder of the American financial system, was one of the nation's ablest statesmen whose friend and mentor had been George Washington. Indignation against Burr for killing him, reinforced by the fact that Hamilton had refused to fire his pistol, forced Burr to flee for his life and ended his political aspirations for good.

Countless deadly encounters took place in Kentucky in the late 1700s and early 1800s. High-profile duelists—such as future President Andrew Jackson (May 30, 1806, in Logan County) and Judge John Rowan, of "My Old Kentucky Home" fame (February 3, 1801, in Nelson County)—added to the mystique of what proponents were fond of calling *code duello*, and intensified its hold over the hotheaded.

Lawmakers tried to curb the practice, but with limited success, because duelists often crossed state lines to avoid the penalties. In fact, many duels fought on Kentucky soil were, in fact, not fought by Kentuckians, as was the case with Jackson, who traveled to Logan County from Nashville, Tennessee, to avoid prosecution by Tennessee authorities.

The problem was so bad by 1795 that one Campbell County resident was moved to submit a notice to a Cincinnati newspaper imploring "the citizens of the North Western Territory to desist from the horrid practice of staining the Kentucky bank of the Ohio River with human gore, by dueling—as it is an open violation of the commonwealth."

BLOOD AND INK

Dueling was especially prevalent among those in the journalism and legal professions, and often hinged on what had been printed in newspapers or said in legislative chambers or courtrooms. Because of this, the general assembly secured passage of a law in 1812 forbidding all "state and judicial officers and attorneys at law" from dueling. It had little effect.

On March 9, 1829, Charles Wickliffe marched into the office of the *Kentucky Gazette* in Lexington demanding that an editor on duty named Benning tell him the author of an item that had recently been published. Benning refused and Wickliffe shot and killed him. Enraged, *Gazette* editor George James Trotter promptly challenged Wickliffe. The two met seven months later, on October 9, near the Fayette County–Scott County border. Trotter avenged Benning, killing Wickliffe at a distance of eight feet.

U.S. Senator and perennial presidential candidate Henry Clay, known as the "Great Compromiser," fought two duels in his lifetime. The first, with Humphrey Marshall, took place after an altercation on the floor of the Kentucky House of Representatives in Frankfort. The men, anxious to avoid legal entanglements, agreed to meet on January 19, 1809, on the Indiana shore across the Ohio River from Louisville. Marshall wounded Clay in the thigh.

Celebrated statesman and presidential candidate Henry Clay fought two duels in his lifetime, neither of which proved fatal. *Courtesy of the Library of Congress.*

Seventeen years later, on April 8, 1826, while serving as U.S. secretary of state, Clay tangled with U.S. Senator John Randolph of Virginia. The two met on the Virginia shore of the Potomac River, opposite Georgetown. Neither man wounded the other, though Clay shot a hole in Randolph's yellow coat. The two were repentant. "You owe me a coat, Mr. Clay," Randolph said, shaking hands with the Kentuckian. "I am glad the debt is no greater," Clay replied.

Congressman Thomas Francis Marshall of Versailles—a grandson of legendary U.S. Supreme Court Chief Justice John Marshall—felt slandered by an item published about him in the *New York Courier and Enquirer*. He challenged the paper's editor, Colonel James Watson Webb, and the two met in Delaware on July 2, 1842. After neither inflicted damage on his opponent in the first round, the belligerents agreed to a second. After the smoke cleared, both men were still standing, but Webb went home with a wound below his left knee.

Others found more creative ways to defend their honor. Two duelists appeared at an Eddyville doctor's office on May 10, 1852, and requested to be bled. The physician opened a vein in each man's arm, and the two bled until each was "pale as a corpse." Thanking the doctor, the men left his office and "pronounced themselves satisfied."

DESCENDING INTO TRIVIALITIES

As mid-century approached, however, dueling began to degenerate into a practice of the young and inebriated, and sometimes for embarrassingly trivial reasons. The state's well-to-do youths, anxious to prove bravery among their inheritances, were quick to challenge one another. The results were often tragic.

In June 1849, prominent Louisville attorneys and lifelong friends John Thompson Gray Jr. and Captain Henry C. Pope were playing cards at the Galt House Hotel. As the evening wore on, Pope became drunk and obnoxious, threatening a fellow poker player with his knife. Gray jumped from his chair, grabbed the knife and threw it out the window. As he attempted to get his friend away from the table to prevent trouble, Pope became so violent that Gray finally felt compelled to hit him over the head with his cane.

The next morning, Pope awoke to find himself cut and bruised. When he learned that his injuries had come at the hands of Gray, he sent the inevitable challenge through Alexander Churchill and Grandison Spratt. Gray's second, Colonel William Preston, implored Churchill and Spratt to help him patch up the friends' differences. Gray even offered to make a public apology, but Pope was unmoved and the duel was set for 10.00 a.m., June 14, on the Indiana shore, six miles north of the city.

Gray had selected shotguns at twenty paces, the "barrels resting in the hollow of the left arm," reported the *Louisville Daily Journal*. The men appeared, and their seconds counted the paces and requested the combatants to turn and fire. Pope fell as the smoke cleared, mortally wounded, "the ball passing through the upper part of his thigh, breaking the bone, and entering the other thigh," according to the *Daily Journal*. The dying man called for his friend and forgave him for their dispute and his impending death. "Gray knelt by him and wept bitterly…'Oh Henry, why didn't you tell me how you felt?'" he sobbed.

The city's newspapers the next morning reported the death of Henry C. Pope as a tragedy, describing in detail the friendship of the men and Gray's attempts to apologize. "What a commentary upon the bloody code of honor!" reported the *Morning Courier*. "Here were two high-minded honorable gentlemen who had been friends from childhood, forced by the bloody code to stand up, and fire at one another, on account of a trivial difficulty which should have been readily adjusted."

Legal Remedy

Many of the state's papers echoed the *Courier*'s outrage, and public indignation remained high when delegates assembled in Frankfort on October 1, 1849, for the state's third constitutional convention.

When the committee of general provisions met, a proposal was made to elevate the 1812 prohibition against dueling by placing it in the new constitution in an attempt to deny duelists from holding public office. The proposal was adopted by the delegates, becoming part of the Kentucky constitution on June 11, 1850. The language was retained in the fourth (and present) constitution, ratified September 28, 1891, which to this day requires officeholders to take the oath that seems so strange to modern ears.

Crittenden

His name is synonymous with compromise, but in a long, successful and ultimately tragic political career, John Jordan Crittenden never compromised on his principles.

Crittenden was born on September 10, 1786, on his father John's vast land holdings near the town of Versailles, in what would become Woodford County. As was the custom for sons of wealthy parents, the young Crittenden attended nearby Pisgah Academy and an area boarding school before beginning the study of law under the direction of an experienced attorney. Crittenden's teacher was family friend George Mortimer Bibb, who would become a U.S. senator, chief justice of the Kentucky Supreme Court and U.S. secretary of the Treasury.

Education

The young man wasn't satisfied with his education, and in an effort to broaden his knowledge, he enrolled at Washington Academy (now Washington and Lee University) in Lexington, Virginia, and later at the College of William and Mary. He learned a Jeffersonian curriculum that stressed Enlightenment philosophers and Republican thought.

Graduating in 1807, Crittenden briefly practiced law in Woodford County before moving to Russellville, county seat of Logan County, which was growing in importance and attracting the attention of aspiring sons of elite Bluegrass families. One of the men he met there was Ninian Edwards who, in eleven years as a lawyer, had served as a judge of the general court of Kentucky, a circuit court judge and an associate and chief justice of the Kentucky Court of Appeals, then the state's supreme court.

An ardent supporter of President Thomas Jefferson, Edwards was appointed governor of Illinois Territory in 1809. He promptly offered his youthful friend the post of attorney general, which Crittenden promptly accepted.

But by 1811, Crittenden felt the pull of Kentucky and returned to Russellville, where he ran a successful campaign for a seat in the state legislature. He also married Sarah O. Lee, with whom he would have seven children.

WAR

Crittenden's budding political career was interrupted by his concern about the crisis between the U.S. and Great Britain over America's maritime sovereignty. With the thought that Kentucky would benefit from his executive and legendary military skills, Crittenden wrote a letter to Isaac Shelby, the state's first governor, urging him to come out of retirement and run for the office again.

Shelby did and trounced his opponent, Gabriel Slaughter, by a nearly three to one margin. Gearing the state up for war, the sixty-two-year-old Shelby made arrangements for Kentucky's defense. After Kentuckians were massacred by British-led Indians at River Raisin, near modern-day Monroe, Michigan, Shelby called for 2,000 volunteers to meet him in Newport to avenge them. More than 3,500 showed up.

Crittenden served as a member of the governor's military staff, in addition to that of General Sam Hopkins. Taking command of the Kentucky army, Shelby led them to victory at the decisive Battle of the Thames, helping to end the war in favor of the United States.

When the two returned home, a grateful Shelby offered a Crittenden a U.S. Senate seat in 1814 before learning that, at twenty-seven, he was too young to serve. Crittenden resumed his legislative career after the war and served as Speaker of the State House in 1815, 1816 and had been elected speaker in 1817 before being chosen to fill a vacant U.S. Senate seat.

FRANKFORT

Leaving the Senate at the end of the term in 1819, Crittenden returned to Kentucky. Realizing that the state capital would offer him more lucrative cases, he moved his practice to Frankfort and quickly became a successful defense and appeals court attorney. He built a reputation that attracted the attention of important clients, including former Presidents James Madison and James Monroe and Henry Clay.

In 1820, Crittenden was appointed, along with John Rowan, to negotiate with Tennessee to end the states' long-standing boundary dispute. Not satisfied when negotiations failed, Crittenden continued to work on the problem. He subsequently recommended a solution to the state legislature, which was accepted by both states.

His reputation as a calming, nonpartisan leader was tested during the Old Court–New Court crisis in the state of the 1820s, as the contending groups divided into parties. Forced to choose, Crittenden took the conservative, Old Court view, which cost him much of his political standing.

Having been elected to the state legislature six consecutive times from Logan County, he found it difficult to win in Frankfort. He was again elected in 1825, but lost in 1826. Winning a special election in 1829, he served until 1832.

Clay

But Crittenden's political fortunes were beginning to change. Having struck up a friendship with Henry Clay, Crittenden became his political manager in the state capital, at a time when state legislatures elected U.S. senators.

Crittenden supported his mentor for the presidency in 1824 and, when the election ended in a stalemate and went to the U.S. House for a decision, he urged Clay to throw his support to John Quincy Adams, who became the nation's sixth president.

When a grateful Adams appointed Clay U.S. secretary of State, the defeated Andrew Jackson charged that Clay had entered into a "corrupt bargain" with Adams to obtain his post. Though apparently untrue, the charge haunted Clay for the rest of his political life.

Death in the Family

After his wife Sarah died, Crittenden married the widowed Mrs. Maria K. Innes Todd, in 1826. The couple would have two children. The new Mrs. Crittenden was considered one of the most beautiful women in Kentucky, which is believed to be one of the reasons Frankfort's Farmers Bank of Kentucky printed the likenesses of the Crittendens on its five-dollar bills.

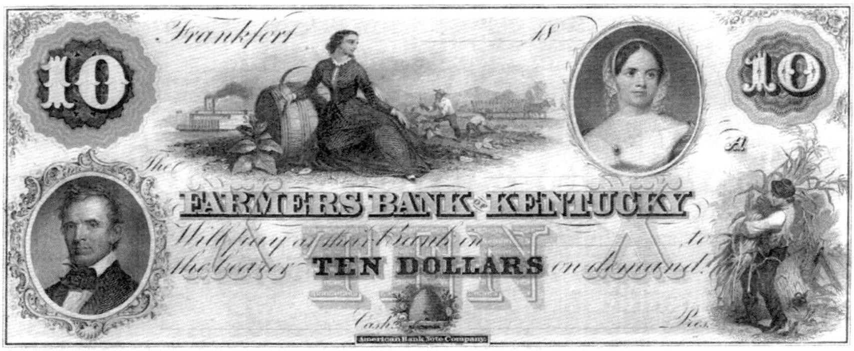

After his first wife's death, Crittenden married the widowed Mrs. Maria K. Innes Todd. When Frankfort's Farmer's Bank of Kentucky used the Crittendens' likenesses on its bills, it was partially because Crittenden was governor at the time. It was rumored that Mrs. Crittenden was included because she was considered one of Kentucky's most beautiful women. *Courtesy of Farmer's Bank of Frankfort.*

President Adams appointed Crittenden a U.S. district attorney in 1827, but he was removed in 1829 when Jackson became president. He was serving as Kentucky secretary of state in 1834 when he was again elected to the U.S. Senate. He served until the end of the term, March 3, 1841, immediately becoming U.S. attorney general under President William Henry Harrison.

But Harrison died in office, and his successor, John Tyler, quickly alienated Clay and the Whig Party. Making a political stand, Crittenden resigned his Senate seat in protest, a move that increased his popularity in Kentucky, where barbecues were held in his honor.

POLITICAL SPLIT

Perhaps to repay Crittenden, the state legislature elected him to Clay's vacated Senate seat, to which he was reelected in 1842.

Supporting Clay for the presidency in 1844, Crittenden agreed with his opposition to Texas annexation. After Clay's defeat, Crittenden also opposed the admission of Texas into the United States, as well as the subsequent Mexican War. Once war began, however, Crittenden supported it and corresponded often with General Zachary Taylor, a kinsman of his first wife. When Taylor's troops won the Battle of Buena Vista, helping to secure American victory, the general became the Whig nominee for the presidency in 1848. Crittenden had a choice to make: support Taylor or alienate Clay, who opposed the general's candidacy. Crittenden supported Taylor, which alienated him from Clay and ended their political association.

In the meantime, Clay introduced legislation that ended a crisis over slavery, resulting in what was known as the Compromise of 1850.

Throwing himself into the effort to elect Taylor, Crittenden pondered the political moves necessary to carry Kentucky for the candidate. He resigned from the Senate to run for governor, securing his state and helping Taylor to gain the presidency. When President-elect Taylor offered him his choice of cabinet positions, however, Crittenden refused them all, perhaps to take office as governor, or perhaps to avoid the appearance of a "bargain." After Taylor died in office in 1850, however, Crittenden almost immediately resigned the governorship to accept President Millard Fillmore's appointment as U.S. attorney general.

Storm Clouds

Crittenden reconciled with Clay before the statesman's death in 1852, but was powerless to stop the death throes of Clay's Whig Party. The politician looked around for another option. He halfheartedly supported the anti-immigrant, anti-Catholic American, or Know-Nothing, Party for a time, but opposed much of its lack of inclusiveness.

Elected to the Senate again in 1854, Crittenden strove against the resurgence of the slavery issue brought about by the Kansas-Nebraska Act, which would extend slavery beyond the South. Assuming Clay's role, he attempted to alleviate sectional tension with conciliation. He spoke thoughtfully and eloquently on the need for compromise and an end to the growing stridency of his fellow senators. Helping found a new Constitutional Union Party, he supported its nominee, John Bell, for president in 1860.

Crisis

In December 1860, a month after Abraham Lincoln's election, Crittenden introduced his Crittenden Compromise proposal to restore and extend the old Missouri Compromise line to the Pacific Ocean. Its terms included that slavery would be protected south and prohibited north of the 36°30' line; new states could decide the slavery questions themselves; and Congress would be prohibited from abolishing slavery in the District of Columbia or regulating the interstate transport of slaves. The proposal was rejected, seven to six, by a special Committee of Thirteen, a group of senators appointed to consider it. Ironically, the defeat of the proposal was secured by a coalition of Southerners and antislavery Republicans.

Crittenden turned to the president-elect—who was Ninian Edwards's brother-in-law—and tried to secure Lincoln's support for his efforts to avert war. Lincoln declined. Refusing to accept the vote of the Committee of Thirteen, Crittenden introduced his proposal to the full Senate. It was rejected twenty-five to twenty-three on January 3, 1861. His Senate term ended two months later.

As South Carolina seceded from the Union and other Southern states lined up to follow, the seventy-four-year-old Crittenden returned to Kentucky and helped keep his state from joining them. He participated in a border-state convention seeking compromise.

FATHER IN THE BROTHER'S WAR

But the Civil War came. Elected to a special session of Congress that met in July 1861, Crittenden secured the passage of resolutions stating that the purpose of the war was to preserve the Union and the Constitution, not to subjugate the South.

George Mortimer Bibb, U.S. senator, chief justice of the Kentucky supreme court and U.S. secretary of the Treasury, was Crittenden's law teacher and friend. The two men named sons after one another. Crittenden's son George Bibb Crittenden, a West Point graduate, became a brigadier general in the Confederate army. *Courtesy of the U.S. Department of the Treasury.*

The momentous crisis tore families apart all across the nation, and Crittenden found himself playing the part of father in the "Brother's War." His son, Thomas Leonidas Crittenden, joined the Union army and rose to the rank of major general. His other son, George Bibb Crittenden, a West Point graduate, went South, becoming a brigadier general.

Crittenden declared his allegiance in an 1862 letter to Thomas. "I am inflexibly for the Union," he wrote. "I can never subscribe to a separation of the United States—It is possible that I may be obliged to submit to it, but I cannot assent to it. It will be in itself, the surrender and (destruction) of our great country."

He died in Frankfort on July 26, 1863.

Making Tracks

It isn't very often that Kentucky is at the forefront of innovation, but in the 1830s it was. The innovation was railroads, and Lexington was home to the second steam-powered railway in the United States.

Founded in pioneer times and dominating the state over the first quarter of the nineteenth century, Lexington began to suffer from its rivalry with the growing Louisville, which was situated on the Ohio River, with its many transportation advantages. Lexington's leaders searched for ways to improve its own transportation assets, in an effort to compete. The city began the state's first "macadamized" (or crushed rock) road in the fall of 1829 to connect it to Maysville and the Ohio River.

The railroad was another improvement. It ran from Lexington to Frankfort, and debuted on January 31, 1834—a short nine years after the opening of the first public railway in the world, in England. The Lexington & Ohio Railway Co. (L&O) was incorporated in Kentucky on January 27, 1830, with $1 million in capital divided into one hundred shares. The company sent a representative to England to examine its railroad, and a Lexington tinkerer named Joseph Bruen set to work fashioning what would become Kentucky's first steam locomotive. The iron rails were placed on a foundation of stone quarried in rectangles two feet wide by up to eight feet long.

The first excursions—designed to generate public interest and support—ran about six miles down the track from Postlewaite's Hotel in Lexington. "[The train] went out to a spring and place of amusement," recalled Dr. Daniel M. Fister, who helped install the rails as a young man. "There were a bowling alley, billiards, refreshment stands, etc."

One year after the line opened, a new engine, affectionately known as the Daniel Boone, took travelers the 28.8 miles to Frankfort in two and a half hours.

MIDWAY

In 1835, the company even built a new town, which served as a stopping point in the middle of the line. Originally called Middleway, it is today's fifth-class city of Midway.

The L&O ran its first train to Louisville in 1851.

A STATEWIDE RAIL LINE

Various railroads were added in Kentucky during the decades prior to the Civil War, but all were small enterprises compared to one: the Louisville & Nashville. Proposed as early as 1836 by Kentucky House Speaker John LaRue Helm of Hardin County, the L&N was founded on March 5, 1850.

Inexperience and mismanagement had forced the effort to the brink of bankruptcy by 1854, and the company's board looked to Helm—who had served as governor from 1850 to 1851—to save it. Elected the company's president, Helm immediately jump-started company fortunes in a campaign-style tour of the proposed route. He pointed out to the citizenry that a rail line from Louisville to Nashville would transform the state's economy, making it a pipeline for goods and raw materials from all across the nation. Helm calmed the fears of jittery investors, secured a new bond issue and even offered to pay assessments due from residents of Hardin County's Meeting Creek community to obtain their support.

According to one Helm tribute, "It was his invincible will, his unquailing grit, his indomitable energy, his signal capacity for affairs, and the public confidence in his ability and integrity, that averted the disaster, pushed the road through to completion and saved it to the stockholders."

The first L&N train traveled between the two cities on October 27, 1859, with Helm aboard. Passenger trips covered the 185 miles in ten hours, three times faster than stagecoaches.

The L&N Railroad was not simply a Louisville entity that facilitated commerce with Nashville; it was a statewide company that would become Kentucky's largest economic engine for decades to come, not only providing access to the South's markets for all Kentuckians, but serving as a kind of transportation linchpin, connecting the state with all points, north, south, east and west.

Disrupted during the Civil War by Confederate raiders who often blew up its bridges, the L&N emerged from the war poised to become one of

Governor John Larue Helm proposed and selflessly championed the cause of a railway connecting Louisville with Nashville. Later helping save the L&N as its president, Helm established a transportation system that remains in place to this day. *Courtesy of Mary Genevieve Murphy.*

the largest and most important transportation companies in the nation. Purchasing and rebuilding former rail lines in the South at a feverish pace, the L&N expanded to the port cities of New Orleans; Mobile, Alabama; and Pensacola, Florida, to the south and to St. Louis, Illinois and Indiana to the west. By the 1890s, it had acquired direct access to Chicago.

Under the leadership of Milton H. Smith, the L&N moved into the coal fields in both eastern and western Kentucky, which also allowed for passenger transportation to Lexington from the state's eastern counties on an unprecedented scale.

TRANSPORTATION REVOLUTION

From the Civil War to 1900, almost all aspects of Kentucky life touched railroads in one way or another, from passenger transportation to freight to mail service. The Cincinnati Southern, Queen and Crescent and Chesapeake & Ohio also began to crisscross the state, until almost every city and town of note was served, and trains were the only way to travel quickly.

Companies often operated special trains at discounted rates during events such as Louisville's Southern Exposition in 1884 and sporting events. Trains even transported soldiers and recruits during the Spanish-American War.

As a young man, Daniel M. Foster of Lexington helped build Kentucky's first railroad. He later became a medical doctor in Missouri.

Passenger prices ranged from fifty cents for a car with wooden benches to several dollars for the white glove treatment in a luxurious Pullman car, complete with comfortable seating, fine dining and overnight accommodations.

Trip to Natural Bridge

Glowing accounts of rail travel were commonplace in 1890s Kentucky newspapers. One example was an 1899 *Lexington Leader* account of an excursion to Natural Bridge for the city's orphans. One hundred of the "unfortunates" boarded a Lexington & Eastern train headed for "the free wilds of nature's healthful haunts!"

"The blue of the sky and the green of the earth lent glorious tints to the shifting panorama of landscape as the summer coach darted by," a reporter wrote, "and not even the smoke of the engine dared to intrude among those rosy child faces at the windows."

Children screamed and laughed whenever the train entered a tunnel and drank lemonade from shiny tin cups. Upon reaching Natural Bridge, they sang "My Country 'Tis of Thee," paying particular attention to the lines "I love thy rocks and rills, thy woods and templed hills." Once back aboard the train, the children sang all the way home—pausing to scream again in all the tunnels.

Political Divisions

The rates rail lines charged were often a sore spot for farmers, who thought companies took too big of a cut into their profits. State Senator William Goebel of Kenton County was only too happy to become their champion, arguing for government price fixing and other limits on the larger rail lines, especially the L&N. Perhaps to counter the negative publicity, the company named one of its trains the "Ellen N.," which was very popular with nineteenth-century travelers.

After engineering passage of a law that gave him power to control the state's elections, Goebel and his allies were able to unseat Governor William S. Taylor and declare Goebel governor. On January 30, 1900, as he prepared to take office, he was shot, dying four days later.

State Senator William Goebel of Kenton County built his career on opposing railroads, especially the L&N. His political posturing made him governor, but also resulted in his assassination. *Courtesy of the Kentucky Historical Society.*

BACK TO THE FUTURE?

Passenger rail service plummeted after World War II, when the federal government began construction of the interstate highway system. Nowadays, trains are mainly in the freight business. The dominant line is CSX, which partially traces its roots to the L&N. Based in Jacksonville, Florida, CSX also owns freight terminals and ocean container shipping companies, the kind that are currently the subject of homeland security debates.

Many state leaders believe the commonwealth of the future will once again ride on rails. Fast-moving light rail systems to move commuters, especially between the cities of the Golden Triangle, would certainly be an improvement over the present system. If the prophecy comes to pass, it will bring trains full circle, important in Kentucky's past, present and future.

Lincoln in Lexington

To hear many national historians tell it, the sum total of Abraham Lincoln's connection to Kentucky was his backwoods birth and boyhood to the age of seven, when his family moved away to Indiana. But there is another story…the true story. From the moment of his birth on February 12, 1809, at the family's Sinking Spring Farm near Hodgenville, to his death on April 15, 1865, the life of the nation's sixteenth president was entwined with his native state.

His boyhood memories were of his father's farm on Knob Creek, in Larue County, and when the Lincolns moved away, they did so with fellow Kentuckians. As he grew, the young Lincoln worked for Kentuckians, borrowed his books from them and was encouraged in his efforts by them.

He recalled earning his "first dollar" ferrying passengers to a steamboat at Pate's Landing in Hancock County, and winning his first court case there in Samuel Pate's house. Lincoln worked for six dollars a month at Taylor's Ferry, the spot where Anderson Creek empties into the Ohio River, and he and his stepbrother John D. Johnston worked as day laborers on Louisville's Portland Canal in 1827. Denton Offutt, owner of the store in New Salem, Illinois, in which the youthful Lincoln worked and first attempted to enter politics, was from Hickman Creek, eight miles southwest of Lexington.

When Lincoln subsequently won a seat in the Illinois legislature as a twenty-three-year-old, it was attorney John Todd Stuart, who was born near Lexington, who loaned him his law books. Stuart became Lincoln's first law partner. It was Mary Owens, visiting her sister from Kentucky, who rejected Lincoln's marriage proposal in 1837.

Lifelong Friendship

On the day he arrived in Springfield, Illinois, on a borrowed horse to begin practicing law with Stuart, Lincoln walked into a furniture store owned by Joshua Fry Speed, placed his saddlebags on Speed's counter and asked the price of "the furniture for a single bedstead." Upon hearing the seventeen-dollar price, Lincoln said, "It is probably cheap enough, but I have not the money to pay. But if you will credit me until Christmas, and my experiment here as a lawyer is a success, I will pay you then. If I fail in that I will probably never pay you at all."

His customer's gloomy tone eliciting pity for him, Speed offered to share his room. "Where is your room?" Lincoln asked. "Upstairs," came the answer. With that, Lincoln wordlessly picked up his saddlebags, walked upstairs and emerged a few minutes later with a smile on his face. "Well, Speed," he said. "I am moved."

Lawyer

Before long, Lincoln was a busy lawyer who spent his free time telling stories in the back room of Speed's store. But at a ball held in honor of the Illinois legislature, everything changed. The twenty-nine-year-old Lincoln met John Todd Stuart's twenty-one-year-old cousin Mary Todd. Though taken with her, the apprehensive Lincoln walked up to her and haltingly said, "Miss Todd. I want to dance with you the worst way." She later recalled that "he certainly did."

Their courtship was an odd one. In many ways, Mary was the exact opposite of Abraham Lincoln. She was charming where he was gawky and clumsy, cultured and educated where he was self-taught. She was a fluent speaker of French who played the piano and had all the social skills taught in the best Lexington homes. He spent his youth at hard labor and had a gift for telling amusing anecdotes.

But they were attracted to one another and the courtship continued, then stopped and then started again. They became engaged, and then Lincoln broke the engagement on New Year's Day 1841. "I am now the most miserable man living," Lincoln told Stuart.

In the hopes that a change of scenery would do him good, Lincoln accepted Speed's invitation to visit his family home near Louisville. It was called Farmington, and Lincoln spent several weeks there that fall, walking its grounds, talking with members of Speed's family and experiencing the kind of life his estranged fiancée knew well. He walked into town almost every morning and lounged around the office of Speed's older brother James, a prominent Louisville attorney. Predictably, he read James's books and spoke with him about their common profession.

Conspiring with Speed, Lincoln accompanied him on the former's often unsuccessful trips to woo Fannie Henning, who lived on a nearby farm in the household of her uncle, John Williamson. Pretending to be a Democrat, Lincoln occupied Williamson so completely that Speed finally had a chance to be alone with Fannie. The two became engaged soon afterward.

But when Speed suffered from forebodings the following year as the date approached, Lincoln counseled him against ending the relationship. Even after Speed was married, Lincoln continuously quizzed his friend about his feelings. Once he determined that his friend was happily married, Lincoln at once decided there was no time to lose.

Early on the morning of November 4, 1842, Lincoln's friend James H. Matheny was awakened by a knock at his door. He opened it to find Lincoln, saying he would be married that night and needed a best man. Lincoln and Mary were married in the home of her sister, Mrs. Elizabeth Edwards, so quickly, it was remembered, that their wedding cake was still warm when guests began to consume it.

Congressman

As a now-successful attorney in Springfield, Lincoln was moving up in the ranks of the local Whig Party, whose majority in the district around Sangamon County was such that it could determine who would serve as the district's congressman. Lincoln thought his standing was enough, and asked for the post. After enduring four years of disappointments, however, it was at last his turn, and he was allowed to run in 1847.

During the campaign, the Whig candidate attended a religious meeting led by his opponent Peter Cartwright, a venerable Methodist minister and noted Democrat. After Cartwright delivered an inspiring sermon, he turned to his congregation and asked anyone wanting to going to heaven to stand. The preacher then asked everyone who didn't want to go to hell to stand. Noting that Lincoln had stood neither time, Cartwright implored the candidate to state where he was going. "If it is all the same to you," he said, "I am going to Congress."

The Lincoln family visited Mary Todd Lincoln's childhood home in 1847 and 1850. Lincoln spent much time in his father-in-law's library there and, in a way, had something of a religious epiphany there. *Courtesy of the Mary Todd Lincoln House.*

On his way to Washington, in mid-October 1847, Lincoln traveled with his family by stagecoach and steamboat to visit Mary's father's Lexington home. Abraham and Mary had two sons by this time, Robert—named for Mary's father—four, and Eddie, one and a half. They spent three weeks there, and Lincoln felt as at home there as he had at Farmington. He awoke late and spent time each morning reading in his father-in-law's library, a place that must have seemed like a wonderland to the former book-starved boy. One of his favorites was *Elegant Extracts, or Useful and Entertaining Passages from the Best English Authors and Translations*. Taking a pencil, he underlined passages he liked and quoted them to family members at dinner.

He underlined a passage from the antislavery poem "Charity," by William Cowper:

But Ah! What wish can prosper, or what prayer
For merchants rich in cargoes of despair,
Who drive a loathsome traffic, gauge and span,
And buy the muscles and the bones of man?

Next to Cowper's "On Receipt of My Mother's Picture," he drew a hand with an index finger pointing to the lines:

Oh that those lips had language! Life has pass'd
With me but roughly since I heard thee last.
Those lips are thine—thy own sweet smile I see,
The same that oft in childhood solaced me.

As he had done during his Louisville visit, Lincoln walked to the courthouse and watched the lawyers and judges try cases. He visited his brother-in-law Levi Todd in his office at Oldham, Todd and Co. in Sandersville and listened to speeches by Dr. Robert Breckinridge and, perhaps, Henry Clay, whom Lincoln called "My beau ideal of a statesman."

On Thanksgiving afternoon, the Lincolns said farewell to the Todds and went on their way to Washington.

In Grief

Three years later, in 1850, mourning the death of their young son Eddie, the family returned to Lexington so Lincoln could help settle the estate of Mary's grandmother Todd, who had died on January 26.

Eddie's death plunged Lincoln into one of his periodic bouts of melancholia, to which he was particularly susceptible. Returning to Robert Todd's library, Lincoln took down a volume titled *The Christian's Defense*. To his surprise, the author related a story that mirrored Lincoln's own youth, when he had read books such as Thomas Paine's *Age of Reason* that had made him something of an agnostic. As he read about this story of Christian conversion, Lincoln became curious about the book's author. Looking at the title page, he found that he was Dr. James Smith, who had once lived in Shelbyville, Kentucky, but who was currently pastor of the Springfield First Presbyterian Church.

Smith had been the preacher at Eddie's funeral.

For the rest of his life, Abraham Lincoln acknowledged his Christian beliefs, especially during his Civil War presidency.

CIVIL WAR

As his presidency began in March of 1861, half the nation had seceded and would soon be in a state of rebellion. Lincoln the politician used all of his powers to find a winning strategy. Kentucky, he decided, was its linchpin.

He enlisted the help of his old friend Joshua Speed and Speed's brother James. Joshua and James became advisers to the president on Kentucky, attending meetings of the state legislature, gauging the public mood and political winds and even purchasing arms for those in sympathy with the Union. James Speed would become U.S. attorney general in 1864.

The president explained his thinking in a letter to Orville H. Browning, a U.S. senator from Illinois who had grown up in Harrison County, Kentucky. "I think to lose Kentucky is nearly the same as to lose the whole game," Lincoln wrote. "Kentucky gone, we can not hold Missouri, nor, as I think, Maryland. These all against us, and the job on our hands is too large for us. We would as well consent to separation at once, including the surrender of this capitol."

With the help of the Speeds, Dr. Robert Breckinridge, Cassius M. Clay Jr. and countless other Kentuckians, Lincoln's desire to save the Union was ultimately achieved.

Mr. Bell's Garden

It isn't uncommon in Lexington in warm-weather months for workers in the various downtown offices to take their lunches to a certain lakeside spot. There, they eat their sandwiches and take their walks amid the natural splendor of giant oaks and poplars, flowering shrubs and lily pads: an hour of tranquility in a busy workday. This idyllic retreat is also a cemetery.

Garden Cemetery

It is Lexington Cemetery, which was founded in 1849. It was designed by Scotsman Charles S. Bell in the "garden" or "rural" style originated by the Père la Chaise Cemetery in Paris and popularized by Mount Auburn Cemetery in Massachusetts. The style consists of curved walkways, numerous trees, shrubs and flowers and often a pond or two in a park-like setting. Bell was hired as superintendent of Lexington Cemetery soon after he designed it and stayed for the next fifty-two years. He built the cemetery on 170 acres of an area known as Boswell's Woods. His "arboretum-type" landscaping features deciduous trees and shrubs and flowering trees designed to bloom throughout Kentucky's growing season.

As Lexington grew, a central cemetery to replace scattered pioneer burial grounds became a priority. Cholera epidemics in the 1830s and '40s made the need even more pronounced. It was an immediate success, attracting the business of the wealthy and influential, who purchased lots for themselves and their pioneer ancestors, whom they reinterred from their original burial sites.

Lexington Cemetery, founded in 1849, was designed in the "garden" style in the pattern of Mount Auburn cemetery in Massachusetts. Despite being a cemetery, it routinely attracts untold numbers of bird-watchers and lovers of trees and flowers, in addition to those simply seeking a pleasant place to pass time. *Courtesy of the author.*

Burial Becomes Icon

The cemetery's crowning glory came in 1851, when senator and presidential candidate Henry Clay—Kentucky's favorite son—accepted the gift of burial sites for his family from John Lutz, who designed the cemetery's walkways, sections and lots. The Great Compromiser had his mother reinterred there that year and expressed his wish to join her.

Clay died in Washington on June 29, 1852, and was brought home to Kentucky by boat and train. Thirty thousand people from all over the state came to pay their respects to "Harry of the West." It is said that when his funeral procession reached the cemetery gates, those at the end of the line were just leaving his home, Ashland, more than two miles away.

By the time Clay was buried, an effort was already underway to construct a "National Monument of Colossal Proportions" in his honor. The result, a $58,000, 120-foot-high monument—designed by Lexington architect and engineer Julius W. Adams—was completed in 1861. Clay and his wife, Lucretia Hart Clay, were interred in its marble sarcophagus upon her death in 1864. The monument serves as the focal point and, to many, the symbol of the cemetery.

Business Boom

Its reputation secure, the cemetery attracted even more business, and became the final resting place for numerous other notable Kentuckians. Vice President John Cabell Breckinridge (1821–1875), at thirty-five the youngest to hold that office in the nation's history, is buried there. So are kinsman Dr. Robert Breckinridge (1800–1871), "founder of the public school system in Kentucky" and an adviser to President Abraham Lincoln; U.S. Senator and U.S. Attorney General John Breckinridge (1760–1806); and Mary Breckinridge (1881–1956), founder of the Frontier Nursing Service in Appalachia.

A tablet in Section A is a monument to William "King" Solomon (1775–1854), a white man who came to Kentucky from Virginia. He was convicted of public drunkenness so many times that a judge ordered him sold into slavery. A free black woman known as "Aunt Charlotte" purchased Solomon for eighteen cents to help her make pies she sold in the city. Long the town drunk, Solomon redeemed himself during the cholera epidemic that killed five hundred people in the summer of 1833. As Lexingtonians fled the city, Solomon dug graves and buried the dead

Kentucky's favorite son, Henry Clay, accepted the offer of a complimentary burial from Lexington Cemetery, making the cemetery popular with the area's well-to-do families. The 120-foot-high Henry Clay monument today serves as a symbol of the cemetery. *Photo by Russell and Sydney Poore.*

for two months, sleeping nights in the cemetery. He was thereafter known as "King" Solomon by grateful citizens who, upon his death, erected the monument in his honor.

Members of the Todd family rest in a shady area in Section F overgrown with flowers and trees. They include General Levi Todd, "an early adventurer to Kentucky and active in its defence in the most perilous times." Todd (1756–1807) was a pioneer and militia major general who fought in the Battle of the Blue Licks and in various Indian campaigns and who later became the first clerk of Fayette County and a member of the first Lexington Board of Trustees and the first state Constitutional Convention. Next to the general lies state Senator Robert Smith Todd (1790–1849) and his wife, Eliza P. Todd, parents of Mary Todd Lincoln.

Others buried in the cemetery include author James Lane Allen, suffragist Frances Beauchamp, legendary UK basketball coach Adolph Rupp, artist Katherine Helm, eye health pioneer Linda Neville, Zachary

The cemetery abounds in beautiful sculpture and interesting tombstones, many with Victorian symbolism and sentiment. *Courtesy of the author.*

Taylor biographer Holman Hamilton, Disciples of Christ church founder "Raccoon John" Smith and Kentucky's first millionaire, John Wesley Hunt.

But true to its roots, the place remains a garden cemetery and, in turn, a wildlife sanctuary. Myriad trees, shrubs and flowers, from sassafras, holly and cypress to Weigela, white crabapple, dahlia Jaunita and red buckeye, can be found there. Birds, squirrels and rabbits abound, often hiding behind tombstones, and ducks feed in two small lakes at the bottom of a shaded hill. Guided "tree walks," in which participants can learn about unusual native and nonnative trees in the cemetery, are held each spring and fall. Audubon Society members have sighted more than 125 bird species on the grounds during bird-watching sessions. Periodic "history walks" consist of tours of the burial sites of the famous and infamous and stories of their lives and contributions.

Victorian sculpture, with its elaborate designs and symbols of sentiment, is everywhere and can bring a tear to the eye even today. A marble baby mattress and pillow support the reclining statue of Frank and Julia Bissicks' two-year-old daughter, Maggie, who died in 1869. A carving of mother and daughter angels ascending into heaven adorns the grave of Sarah Anderson McClelland and her child, who died in 1852. Other tombstones display urns, lambs, cherubs and crosses in stone, symbolic of remembrance and faith.

The unusual idea of combining a garden with a cemetery has brought together the living and dead for more than 150 years.

Liquid Bluegrass

Bourbon. It has been called the quintessential American drink. Kentucky is not only its birthplace, but also its home.

Like many inventions, bourbon is said to owe its origins to an accident. Baptist minister Elijah Craig, who built a thriving settlement around what came to be known as the Royal Spring in present-day Georgetown, distilled whiskey, among many other enterprises. One day, so the story goes, the staves that would form his barrels were accidentally scorched by fire. Deciding to use them anyway on the inside of the barrels, Craig found that this whiskey, upon aging, had a better flavor, in addition to a pleasing amber color.

True or not, it is a fact that Kentucky's version of what Scots-Irish frontiersmen called "usquebaugh" (pronounced whis-kee-bah) became famous and somehow associated with Bourbon County.

Bourbon versus Whiskey

But what is bourbon—and just what sets it apart from your everyday whiskey? By rule and international agreement, bourbon must be made from 51 percent to 79 percent corn and aged a minimum of two years in new white oak barrels, charred on the inside. Most bourbons are aged between four and eight years, picking up their distinctive flavoring characteristics as they pass through the charred wood as the seasons change.

The essential ingredient that makes bourbon unique is Kentucky's limestone-filtered water, which removes minerals such as iron that adversely affect taste. When everything is combined, the result is pure Kentucky.

True to its legend, all bourbon must be aged at least two years in white oak barrels charred on the inside. *Courtesy of the Buffalo Trace Distillery.*

OIL OF DEMOCRACY

Such perfection gained notice as early as the 1830s, when Henry Clay—Speaker of the U.S. House, U.S. senator and presidential candidate—began bringing bourbon to Washington, where it quickly gained a loyal following among the nation's leaders. Presidents Andrew Jackson and Ulysses S. Grant were particular fans, as were writers Mark Twain, Rudyard Kipling and Walt Whitman.

Historian and critic Bernard DeVoto once wrote that bourbon was a tremendous aid to democracy. "Taken without ice by American patriots," he said, "[it] quickens the political processes, disperses doubts and shadows, and helps men of good will to resolve their differences."

And the tradition lives on. A 1990s study determined that, per capita, seven times more bourbon is consumed in Washington, D.C., than any other place in the nation.

New York

Another hotbed of bourbon enthusiasm has long been New York City. In the 1890s, well-heeled devotees were fond of meeting in the old Waldorf Hotel bar, which featured polished wood, elks' heads and a seductive painting, *The Ballet Dancer*. Carafes of water adorned each table, allowing patrons to arrive at the mixture of bourbon and water that suited their tastes. Regulars included General Nelson A. Miles, U.S. Army chief of staff; New York political boss and U.S. Senator Thomas Collier Platt; Admiral Robley D. "Fighting Bob" Evans; *New York World* correspondent Richard Harding Davis; Stephen Crane, author of *The Red Badge of Courage*; and, on occasion, Henry Watterson of the *Louisville Courier-Journal*.

A few blocks away was the Hoffman House—with its seventy-five-foot-long bar and Bouguereau masterpiece *Nymphs and Satyr*—the watering hole of future President Grover Cleveland; circus showman P.T. Barnum; publisher William Randolph Hearst; and the legendary William F. "Buffalo Bill" Cody, who once remarked when offered a glass of Kentucky's finest, "Sir, you speak the language of my tribe."

Kentucky's Legacy

As a commodity and symbol of the state, bourbon quickly came to be a prized possession of Kentucky's statesmen, and they took great care to see that it remained so. As the frontier moved westward, bourbon moved with it—in barrels. Saloonkeepers, anxious to maintain their stocks of the beloved product, began diluting it with water, prune juice and even fusel oil, a poisonous byproduct of incomplete distilling.

After overhearing a doctor remark that if a quality-assured medicinal whiskey went on the market it would sell for a premium price, twenty-four-year-old Louisvillian George Garvin Brown went to work to provide one—helping to solve part of the adulterated bourbon problem in the process. Brown began bottling his medicinal whiskey, which he soon began calling Old Forester, in 1870. This began Brown-Forman Corp., today a worldwide company still based in Louisville. But the overall problem persisted into the 1890s. A Congressional investigation determined that, of the 107 million gallons produced in 1896, only 2 million hadn't been diluted.

"The ancient Bourbon flavor had departed," wrote Edmund H. Taylor of Frankfort, "and the stomach groans under the dominion of the new ruler." Taylor—a successful distiller, businessman and great-nephew of President Zachary Taylor—began lobbying Congress for relief. He found a willing ally in John Griffin Carlisle of Kenton County, who just happened to be secretary of the U.S. Treasury.

The resulting legislation was the Bottled-in-Bond Act of 1897, which provided for uniform manufacturing standards that ensured product purity, in addition to the once-familiar green paper bottle seals that bore Carlisle's likeness.

The perfect mint julep. *Courtesy of* Kentucky Monthly *magazine.*

Bourbon-making flourished in Kentucky, with thousands of distillers operating almost anywhere limestone water could be found. Irish immigrant James Ripy built upon his enterprise in Tyrone, in Anderson County, until, by 1875, it was the largest "sour mash" distillery in the United States. Labels also flourished, from the familiar Old Crow, Early Times and Jim Beam to the not-so-familiar Old Cobweb, Kentucky Velvet and Medley Brothers.

Near-death Experience

The Eighteenth Amendment to the Constitution outlawed the manufacture or consumption of alcoholic beverages after January 17, 1920. Known as the Prohibition Act, the legislation put tens of thousands of Americans out of work and ended the prolific aspect of distilling in Kentucky for all time.

One provision of the new law allowed for the issuing of ten U.S. Treasury Department permits to sell bourbon as medicine. Acting quickly, Brown-Forman Corp. and Edmund H. Taylor's Ancient Age distillery secured two of these permits, keeping their companies intact and helping preserve the existence of bourbon. Needing a steady supply, Brown-Forman bought the Early Times brand and prepared for the future.

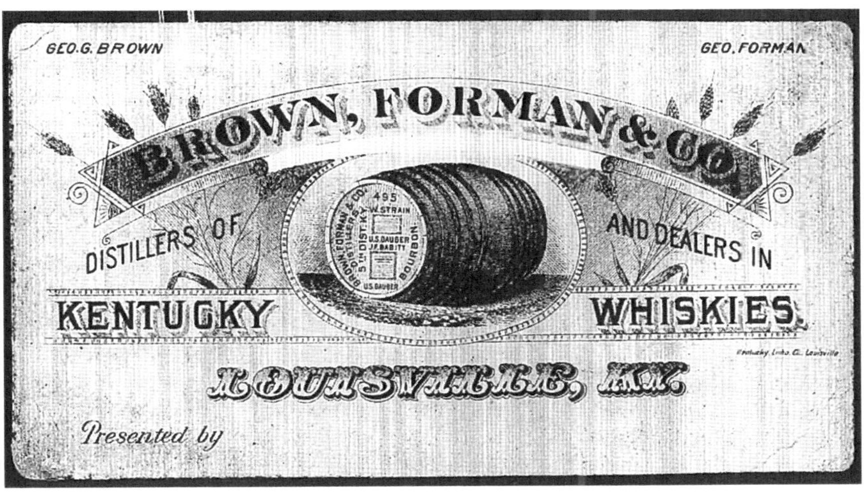

An early salesman's card from the Brown-Forman Corp., founded in Louisville in 1870 by George Garvin Brown. It was one of the first to produce, market and distribute bourbon beyond the borders of Kentucky. The company remains one of the leaders in the beverage industry. *Courtesy of* Kentucky Monthly *magazine.*

But times were simply not good for bourbon. Even after the repeal of Prohibition in 1933, it was almost impossible to obtain. World War II made the problem worse because many of the nation's distillers had converted to the production of industrial alcohol for the war effort. By the end of the war, public tastes had moved away from straight bourbon. Reasoning that customers would return to their former habits, however, Brown-Forman built a new Early Times distillery in Louisville and emphasized production of the brand. The gamble paid off. Returning to the market in 1949, it soared in popularity as Americans demanded premium products in the burgeoning consumer economy. By 1953, Early Times was the number one straight bourbon in the United States. It also became Brown-Forman's biggest seller and top income producer.

Other brands, such as Ancient Age, Jim Beam and Four Roses, also built loyal national followings.

RISE OF THE PREMIUMS

Traditionally, bourbons aged in various barrels were blended to provide a flavor consistent with their respective brands. Buffalo Trace Distillery in Frankfort changed all that in 1984 with its Blanton's brand, which became the first commercial single-barrel bourbon. In response to consumer demand for anything authentic, single-barrel bourbons are now all the rage, along with premium brands of blended bourbons, such as Woodford Reserve, Knob Creek and Booker Noe's.

As in the past, however, there are critics who say Kentucky would be better off without its liquid icon. Graves County native Alben Barkley, who served as vice president under Harry S. Truman, was once on the side of prohibitionists, but mellowed in his assessment of bourbon. "If you don't use it too much," Barkley said, "it will never hurt anyone."

Abraham Lincoln—whose father once worked as a barrel maker for a distiller—could only agree. "If people are injured," Lincoln wrote, "the injury arises not from the use of a bad thing, but from the abuse of a very good thing."

THE MINT JULEP

The mint julep was invented—or at least perfected—by J. Soule Smith of Lexington, who published its recipe in small presentation booklets. By tradition, the julep is made with mint leaves in their natural state and a syrup made of sugar, ice and bourbon.

The julep cup appeared in Kentucky as early as 1816. The best were made of melted silver coins in Lexington by Asa Blanchard, who operated a shop at Mill and Short Streets from 1810 to 1838. Julep cups are still presented by Churchill Downs as a trophy for some races at the track, including the Kentucky Oaks.

Louisville *Courier-Journal* editor Henry Watterson—famous as much for being a Kentuckian as for anything else—was often asked for his julep recipe. "Pluck the mint gently from its bed, just as the dew of the evening is about to form upon it," Watterson directed. "Select the choicer sprigs only, but do not rinse them. Prepare the simple syrup and measure out a half-tumbler of whiskey. Pour the whiskey into a well-frosted cup. Throw the other ingredients away and drink the whiskey."

Like bluegrass, however, the julep is something non-Kentuckians just don't seem quite able to grasp. When celebrated writer H.L. Mencken—a Marylander by birth—was quoted as saying he made his julep with crushed mint and rye whiskey, humorist and Kentuckian Irvin S. Cobb was incensed. "Any guy who'd put rye in a mint julep and crush the leaves," Cobb wrote, "would put scorpions in a baby's bed."

The Shakers

On January 1, 1805, three missionaries from the Society of Believers—commonly called Shakers—set off from their warm, comfortable homes in New Lebanon, New York, for the wilds of Kentucky. Their names were Benjamin Youngs, Issachar Bates and John Meacham, and they had reason to believe they would be sowing the seeds of their beliefs in fertile fields. This westernmost portion of the United States called Kentucky—only thirteen years removed from statehood—had become a melting pot of sorts for religion. Pioneering clergymen were seeing the masses streaming into the new commonwealth as potential converts, and they competed with one another to win as many souls for their churches as possible.

A Spark

Baptist preachers, Methodist circuit riders and Presbyterian ministers worked tirelessly to bring their faiths to the new land, while whole congregations pulled up stakes in Virginia or elsewhere to follow the westward settlements. Into this cauldron of religious zeal was thrown the spark of an idea: a meeting—a revival meeting.

It occurred in August 1801 at Cane Ridge, in Bourbon County. As many as twenty thousand people—an immense number for the time—gathered amid a cacophony of preachers continuously extolling their faiths for days on end. It has been called one of the most important events in American religious history.

Cane Ridge was a kind of religious mall in which the ripe-for-the-picking pioneers could sample various beliefs before deciding on which one to adopt. The crowds were said to have been remarkably open-minded, ready to listen to almost any religious theory and accept any number of new ways to reconcile with God.

The effect of this sensory overload was at once glorious and frightening. People screamed, sang, danced or prayed incessantly. Attracting the most attention, however, was the phenomenon of body-shaking among the crowd. It came to be known as "jerking" or "the jerks," and was widely reported. Written accounts of Cane Ridge convinced Shaker leaders that a profoundly important religious realignment was taking place in what was at the time called the West.

KENTUCKY

"The Shakers could not have chosen a better time to come to Kentucky," said Sharon Duane Koomler, director of the Shaker Museum and Library in Old Chatham, New York. "What a remarkable journey: Three men starting out walking to where they knew not where. I have come to admire them tremendously."

As Youngs, Bates and Meacham journeyed through the severest winter in more than two decades, they went from neighborhood to neighborhood in Ohio and Kentucky, seeking to win converts to their belief. Convincing pioneers to accept church founder Mother Ann Lee, whom the Shakers

This modest meetinghouse in Cane Ridge in Bourbon County was a landmark religious epicenter in 1801. *Courtesy of the Library of Congress.*

believed was Christ's second coming in female form, seems a tall order to modern minds. Shakers also had to induce commitments from potential converts—even married ones—to renounce "the flesh" and become celibate for the remainder of their lives.

In the aftermath of Cane Ridge, they found many willing to accept their new doctrine. By August 1805, they had forty-four adults willing to sign a covenant to start a new Shaker settlement at Shawnee Run, a 140-acre Mercer County farm owned by Elisha Thomas. The members agreed to a communal existence, with property owned by the entire group.

By 1812, the Shakers had acquired more than 4,300 acres and more than one hundred members, moved to Pleasant Hill and boasted three communal "families," which they called East, Centre and West, in addition to a convert settlement. With a strong work ethic and legendary resourcefulness and ingenuity, the Shakers flourished, becoming not only self-sufficient but also profoundly successful in virtually anything they tried, from stock-raising and seed cultivation to interior design and woodworking.

A New Architecture

Twenty-three-year-old Micajah Burnett, who had been brought into the society at age seventeen, in 1809, designed and built most of the architecturally beautiful buildings that made the settlement what it was. By 1830, Pleasant Hill had a population of five hundred, and the Shakers lived and worked on more than four thousand acres and in hundreds of beautiful and, in many cases, architecturally notable buildings.

The magnificent Trustee's House at Pleasant Hill, designed by Micajah Burnett, who was twenty-three years old when he began designing the community's buildings. *Courtesy of Shaker Village of Pleasant Hill, Harrodsburg, Kentucky.*

In the 1960s, a not-for-profit group led by Earl D. Wallace formed to restore and interpret Pleasant Hill's history as a tourist attraction. Attracting about 250,000 visitors annually to more than thirty restored buildings, it is one of Kentucky's best historic preservation success stories. *Courtesy of Shaker Village of Pleasant Hill, Harrodsburg, Kentucky.*

DECLINE

New members were hard to come by. Often, the only people interested were the destitute who came for the room and board they could obtain. Many, unwilling to live according to Shaker principles, soon left. Orphans adopted into the community often left upon becoming adults.

The Civil War and a series of congregational splits brought the population to about 170 by 1880. The last Pleasant Hill Shaker, Mary Settles, died there in 1923.

RESTORATION

Shakertown looked much like a small Kentucky village with interesting architecture by the early 1960s, when a not-for-profit group led by Earl D. Wallace formed to restore and interpret its history as a tourist attraction. Raising money and learning as they went, members opened eight buildings at Shakertown in 1968.

Under the leadership of James C. Thomas, who retired in 2005, Shakertown became one of Kentucky's best historic preservation success stories, attracting about 250,000 visitors annually to more than thirty restored buildings. It is the largest Shaker restoration in the United States.

The President and the First Lady

In 1883, a man named Alfred Francis Russell was sworn in as president of Liberia. This fairly routine transfer of executive authority attracted little attention outside Monrovia, capital of the West African nation founded in 1847 by freed American slaves. Outside of diplomatic circles, the event was virtually unknown in the United States. Only Russell, it seems, knew just how far he had come—and even he probably didn't know all the particulars.

The new president's incredible story began with his great-grandfather, Colonel John Todd, one of the wealthiest men in Kentucky and one of its frontier leaders. It was August 1782 and Indians under the renegade Simon Girty had laid siege to the fort at Bryan's Station. Militiamen from the Lexington fort, including Todd, rushed to help their fellow pioneers, an act that led to their defeat at the Battle of the Blue Licks on August 19, 1782.

Todd left a widow, Jane, and an infant daughter, Mary Owen Todd, living inside the fort. By the time she was eighteen, Mary's inheritance made her one of Kentucky's richest women. Not surprisingly, she was quickly married to Colonel James Russell, and the couple had a son named after his well-remembered maternal grandfather, John Todd Russell.

A widow herself by the time young John was two, Mary Todd Russell lived on a choice spot among her nearly two thousand acres of Kentucky bluegrass, "in a fine old colonial mansion…in the most elegant style." She lived, however, for her son and spent her time carefully looking after his growth and education. On the verge of adulthood, John Todd Russell was described as a person of "rare charm," having a "striking personal appearance, over six feet in height, unassuming, generous, amiable."

As he prepared to enter Princeton in the fall of 1816, the young man spent the summer with his maternal grandmother, the widow of John

Alfred Francis Russell, a great-grandson of Kentucky pioneer Colonel John Todd and son of John Todd Russell and his grandmother's mulatto servant, Milly, became president of Liberia in 1883. *Courtesy of* Kentucky Monthly *magazine.*

Todd, who by this time was also the widow of Thomas Irvine. Mrs. Irvine had a beautiful, well-educated fifteen-year-old house servant named Milly, who "bore little evidence of her Ethiopian blood." John and Milly soon formed what was called a "secret but ardent attachment" that lasted throughout the summer.

His vacation over, John left for Princeton—presumably not knowing that Milly had become pregnant with his child. Milly delivered a "fine sturdy boy" the following spring, "as fair in complexion as any white child in Kentucky." He was named Alfred Francis.

After two years away at Princeton, John Todd Russell abandoned his studies and returned to Kentucky, the wealth of his family allowing him to take his place in its society. But a long life of happiness was not to be his. While returning home to Lexington from Gallatin County in October 1822, Russell became violently ill in Shelbyville. Knowing that he was near death, Russell's thoughts turned to his young son. Wanting to "insure the freedom and respectability of the child," Russell "acknowledged Milly's boy Alfred to be his son." Then he died.

Russell's inconsolable mother Mary desperately wanted her son's family with her, but in slavery times, this required satisfying the claims of their "owners" besides her mother. Mary frantically tried to purchase Milly and Alfred and was unmercifully taken advantage of, eventually paying "the enormous sum" of $1,200.

Mary brought Milly and Alfred into her home and treated them virtually as members of the family. Alfred was a "bright, lovely, well-behaved lad." But like the illegitimate son of a king in earlier times, Alfred would be unable to secure his inheritance, and Mary made arrangements to send him and his mother to freedom in Liberia.

But when Mary Todd Russell married Robert Wickliffe, one of the richest men in the state, all her plans unraveled. Under Kentucky law, the moment she became Wickliffe's wife, her slaves—though not her land and other property—were conveyed to him. Betraying his reason for marrying her in the first place, Wickliffe refused to free Milly and Alfred unless his wife signed over her fortune to him. He "extorted from her a conveyance of all her property," the deeds of which she signed on September 12, 1827. Having given everything she had to secure her grandson's freedom, Mary quickly sent him and his mother to Liberia. It was related that "the last reputed descendant of John Todd, if he still lives, is in poverty on the barbarous shores of Africa."

The above quotes were the contentions of Mary Owen Todd Russell Wickliffe's cousin, Robert Smith Todd, in a lawsuit he filed against Wickliffe after Mary's death. Todd—an attorney who had handled Mrs. Wickliffe's finances before she signed them over to her husband—sued Wickliffe for the return of Mary's property to the Todd family. When Robert S. Todd died on July 16, 1849, the Todd family was represented by the husband of his daughter Mary Ann, a lawyer and congressman. His name was Abraham Lincoln.

For his part, Wickliffe denied that his wife had given him her Todd family property for any reason other than "love and affection." Furthermore, Wickliffe contended, Robert Todd had revived an "old and long forgotten tale" to gain a legal advantage, pushing his wife into "an untimely grave."

Wickliffe also disputed that Alfred was impoverished. "He is now, I am informed, a respectable Methodist divine, and a perfect gentleman in his manners. When Monrovia…was attacked," he added, "he stood the powder and shot of the enemy and fought in her defense most bravely."

When the Lincolns left Lexington so Abraham could return to Congress, the court case continued in other hands. Wickliffe subsequently prevailed.

History, of course, had much in store for the Lincolns. Mary Todd Lincoln became first lady, living an excruciating existence as she watched

First Lady Mary Todd Lincoln and Liberian President Alfred Francis Russell were second cousins. It is unlikely that either knew the full story of their kinship. *Courtesy of* Kentucky Monthly *magazine.*

the nation—and the Todds—torn apart by the Civil War. Enduring the assassination of her husband and the deaths of two of her sons, she became a tragic, eccentric figure, living in something of a fantasy world in her sister's house in Springfield, Illinois, until she died in 1882.

Her second cousin, Alfred Francis Russell, was sworn in as president of Liberia the following year and died in office in April 1884. It is unlikely either one knew the entire story of their kinship.

The College Experience

As fall 1879 approached, the men of Kentucky University—traditionally known as Transylvania—became interested in the game of football, which was being played by college students like themselves in the East. Considering themselves a campus football "club," the men of KU began practicing, meanwhile encouraging their counterparts at Danville's Centre College to do the same. Centre was subsequently issued a challenge to meet KU's football club at Lexington's City Park the following April 9. In a game lasting from 4:00 to 6:00 p.m., attracting an estimated five hundred spectators, KU beat Centre 13¾ to 0.

"It was pronounced that foot-ball had decidedly the advantage of base-ball as a mean of amusement to the spectators," wrote a reporter for the *Lexington Daily Transcript*. "The collisions between players at various times were almost equal to the coming together of two Spanish bulls, and provoked much laughter."

It was the first intercollegiate football game played in Kentucky.

A New Rival

The Agricultural and Mechanical College of Kentucky—which had been part of KU until the Kentucky General Assembly separated the two schools in 1878—was moving to its new campus on South Limestone, with a fresh new name: Kentucky State College. It was a quasi-military school, which placed particular emphasis on training civil and mechanical engineers, and was said to be undergoing a "meteoric shower of new students," swelling its roll to more than 250.

When the cooling autumn weather of 1881 turned the attention of the KU men to football, they challenged their former schoolmates, who had come to be known as the "Cadets," to a series of three intercollegiate contests. The challenge—including the rule that players had to be under seventeen years old—was accepted and the first game was scheduled for Saturday, November 12.

Game day dawned drizzly in central Kentucky and the *Lexington Daily Transcript* noted that the teams had "rather a slippery day" for their game that afternoon. The Cadets arrived at the "Old Fair Grounds" with fifteen players. This was an acceptable number under Australian rules, upon which local football is said to have been based. They included "Tolbert, Clark, Bartlett, Lee, DeRoode, Seibricht, Downing, Farrell, Fyffe, Elliot, Parker, Irvine, Morgan and Downing."

In "quite an exciting game," the Cadets triumphed by a score of 7½ to 1, which is somewhat unclear because fractions weren't used in Australian football. "The football club is jubilant over its success, and the boys continue to practice the art of kicking," reported the *Transcript.* "They often practice on each other's seats."

Elsewhere in the paper, a reporter predictably tried to pull competitiveness back toward academics. "If the State College and Kentucky University want to get up something more interesting than a football match, they should get up a spelling match between fifty picked men from each school. The people would take a great interest." The Transylvania correspondent conceded that a spelling contest would be popular but questioned "how many of the University boys would risk a public demonstration of their ignorance."

Athleticism prevailed, however, and the teams agreed to a return match the following Saturday, November 19. Despite their loss, Transylvania reported that "the usual amount of foot-ball excitement again rages, and as a natural consequence there is an increased demand for new shirts and 'arnics.'" Transy's team members were "Clay, Davidson, Harris, Hinton, Thurgood, Rogers, McDonald, Macay, Ballou, Knight, McGarvey, Dunlap, Hunt, Phillips and Winn."

"Justice being given to all," noted a Transylvania partisan, "we can bespeak a close game for our boys." The prophesy proved correct, with KSC falling 2 to 1.

The rubber match would be on December 3. The *Transcript* notice read: "There will be another match game of foot-ball between the University

Club and the State College Club at the Old Fair Grounds next Saturday afternoon, beginning at 2 o'clock. Every body invited—particularly the ladies. Admission free."

As game time neared, the newspaper again tried to drum up attendance for "that scientific and rare game, foot ball…Of course all places of business will be closed, and the entire city will turn out to enjoy this rare treat."

"These contests develop muscle wonderfully," said a *Transcript* reporter, "and if not carried too far, are admirable accomplishment for hard study. Play a fair, gentlemanly game, my hearties, but work for all that's in you." KSC lost to its cross-town rival again, 3¼ to 2¼, ending its inaugural season with a 1–2 record.

A New Beginning

Football of the intercollegiate brand died out for a decade until 1891, when KSC challenged Georgetown College to a contest. The first game of KSC's football reemergence was held on April 10, 1891, in a contest billed as the "State championship and…the event of the season." The teams played on Transylvania's field in a struggle that was "exciting and witnessed by a large crowd." KSC won 6 to 2. The following school year—but still considered the same season—KSC scheduled an away game at Transylvania and a home contest against Danville's Centre College. It was a challenge game that included a fifty-dollar prize to guarantee the visitors' appearance.

The Transy game was canceled after a player was injured, so the KSC partisans went back to Limestone Street and began preparing for Centre. On December 18, the night before the contest, "an enthusiastic crowd" met in the chapel. The group elected civil engineering Professor James P. Nelson its chairman and W.S. Page secretary. Professor J.W. Newman, noting the long-standing disagreement between the all-male Patterson Literary Society and the all-female Philosophian literary society over school colors, announced that the faculty "had decided to settle that question."

Football player Richard C. Stoll recalled that blue was suggested, and "someone on the other side of the chapel said, 'What color blue will it be?'" "I happened to have on a blue necktie and took it off and held it up," Stoll said. "That was the color blue which was adopted…The blue at the University is a peculiar color of blue, but it so happened that was

Richard C. Stoll suggested blue as the University of Kentucky's primary color in 1893 as a member of the football team, taught law there in the early 1900s and served almost continuously on the Board of Trustees from 1898 until his death in 1948, usually as chairman of its executive committee. His was the only portrait of a non-UK president ever to hang in the Board of Trustees Room. *Courtesy of Special Collections & Archives, University of Kentucky.*

the color in my necktie." Next morning, the *Transcript* reported that state college's colors were "dark blue and light yellow. A motion was made that the colors selected be adopted, which was carried by a big majority." The meeting-goers also adopted a "college yell," which after quite a bit of discussion, turned out to be: "Rah! Rush! Ree! A! M!! C!!!"

Tom Shelby was granted possession of the colors. "The home team is now ready for Old Centre's renowned [sons] who have won several victories of late," the *Transcript* reported the next morning. "When the sun goes down to-night we predict for our boys a great victory. This game will certainly decide the championship of the South. The two teams have never been defeated, and the friends are waiting anxiously the result."

Shelby took the school colors to the "C.S. Depot," where they were escorted to the Lexington baseball park, the site of the game. "The State College boys appeal to Lexington friends to put on their colors, and witness the battle, as a large delegation of Danville people will be on hand to back their men."

The *Danville Advocate* noted that the 3:30 p.m. start time was decided to allow Centre's players and friends the opportunity to travel to Lexington on the "accommodation train," which left Danville at 1:16 p.m. Travelers were charged $1.40 for a round-trip ticket, which the railroad company promised to reduce to $1.05 if at least fifty tickets were sold, "which will doubtless be the case."

The *Advocate* reported several changes in Centre's veteran lineup. "Turner, Cheek and Edwin Van Winkle will be unable to play." To take their places were "Swope, Barbour and Arthur VanWinkle, members of the Junior Eleven, and three good men." The paper said changes had also been made in the positions players would play. "Captain Berry will here after play full back entirely, as this will give him a better command of his men."

The Centre starters were "Hudson, right end; Swope, right tackle; Boyer, right guard; Allen, center guard; Willin, left guard; Barbour, left tackle; Douglass, left end; A. Van Winkle, quarter back; Cook, right half back; Hardin, left half back; Berry (Capt.) full back." KSC started Wheat, center rush; Ed Hobdy, right tackle; Colyer, right guard; Ulysses Garrard, left guard; King, tackle; Sturgil, left end; Norman, right end; John Bryan, right half back; Ferrington (captain), left half back; Wallis, quarter back; and Brent, full back.

"Nearly a thousand people" showed up at the baseball park to witness the contest, reportedly "the hardest fought game ever played in the State." The team from Centre, however, didn't arrive at the train depot until 3:00 p.m. and by the time the visitors were ready to take the field, it was almost 4:00 p.m. They were dressed in their orange and black "suits" that "showed the 'earth-earthy' nature of their favorite sport, and were considerably the worse for wear."

The blue and white streamer tradition was continued in the 1920s in the form of a car parade. *Courtesy Special Collections & Archives, University of Kentucky.*

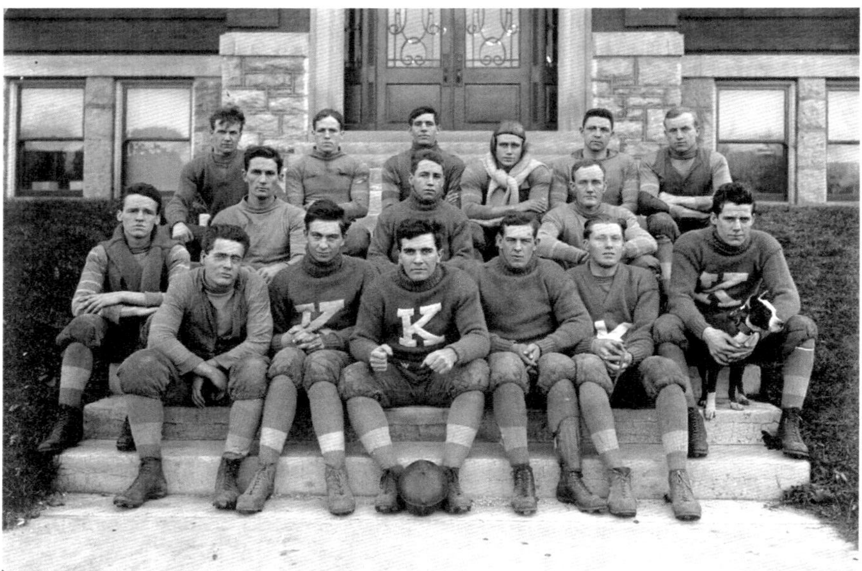

The 1909 KSC football team, whose win over Illinois changed the school's nickname from Cadets to Wildcats. *Courtesy Special Collections & Archives, University of Kentucky.*

Centre chose "Mr. Blaine of Danville" for referee, while Dwight Harrison was the Cadet's choice at "umpire." The visitors unleashed a mighty running game against KSC, with Douglass and Hardin "beat the record on runs and dodging." KSC's Hobdy, Brent, Wallis and Bryan slowed the onslaught, and several of their hard-hitting tackles prompted "loud and long" yells from the Lexingtonians. The *Transcript* also reported that "the young ladies seemed to enjoy the game and applauded every effort of the home team."

The squads battled until darkness, when the game was called. The score was Centre 10, KSC 0. "The home boys were placed at many disadvantages," said the *Transcript* reporter. "They had received but two weeks training, while the Centre College boys have had constant drills since September."

Still, the Lexington team impressed everyone. "Many of the best posted men say that [the] State College boys need a little more practice," said the *Transcript*. "Even the Centre College men complimented are boys by saying their efforts were magnificent."

But the most important knowledge the Centre players had learned from their trip, wrote the *Transcript* reporter, was that Lexington was the "home of more pretty girls than all other Kentucky towns combined."

The following year, KSC changed its colors to blue and white, its nickname to Wildcats in 1909 and, in 1917, its name to the University of Kentucky.

Henry Clay's Great-granddaughter

Each election day thousands of Kentucky women go to the polls and cast their ballots for offices ranging from city commissioner to county judge to president of the United States. But it wasn't always this way. Before 1920, most American women couldn't vote in state and national elections. That right was won for them in a seventy-two-year struggle that began at a women's rights conference in Seneca Falls, New York, in 1848.

In Kentucky, much of the credit belongs to Madeline McDowell Breckinridge, a great-granddaughter of Henry Clay, who worked toward the goal for more than twelve years. As president of the Kentucky Equal Rights Association (KERA, not to be confused with the Kentucky Education Reform Act) beginning in 1912, Breckinridge used her considerable oratorical skills, powerful social standing and her husband's *Lexington Herald* newspaper to further the cause.

Women's Rights

Kentucky during the period was at a crossroads in more ways than one. With strong Union sympathies during the Civil War, it was said to have seceded afterward. Confederate veterans dominated statewide offices, including the governorship, until at least 1895.

If married, women had no parental rights over their own children, could not control real estate they owned prior to marriage and had limited legal rights to any income they might earn. The home, according to the lofty male theory of the time, was the most important aspect of existence, and a woman's place was in her home presiding over it and rearing and

Madeline McDowell Breckinridge, a great-granddaughter of Henry Clay, used her formidable political skills to help secure the right to vote for Kentucky's women. *Courtesy of Dr. Melba Porter Hay.*

educating her children, activities many regarded as women's noble—and Biblical—duty. Low, grimy pursuits, such as politics and business, were best left to men.

Breckinridge wrote,

> *The Southern gentleman is back in the Middle Ages when it comes to chivalry. He believes in other men protecting their women as he protects*

> *or would fight if it were demanded to protect his women. He overlooks the fact that some women may not have a chivalrous man individual to protect her or to fight for her or for himself.*
>
> *I have noticed in the tales of chivalry...the lady for whom the Knight fought was always noble, young and beautiful, never plebian, old or ugly. Who protected the plain, old and ugly woman, I wonder? Who...protected the peasant women and the women who did not rank as "ladies" in those times, climes, and social strata?...There are factory girls in the South, children, women who have no knights to fight for them, but many to oppress them. Therefore, I hold, that these women must, by law, by the vote, protect themselves.*

But Kentucky wasn't as "Southern" in regard to voting as might be imagined. Widows and women with dependent children could vote in some elections as early as 1838, though many didn't or wouldn't. The 1894 bill creating second-class cities in Kentucky allowed all women in Lexington, Newport and Covington to vote in school elections.

A Spark

The great spark for women's suffrage in Kentucky, however, occurred in 1902, when the state legislature removed female voting from the second-class cities law. The result was a groundswell of support for KERA, the women's rights organization founded in 1888 by Laura Clay, daughter of Cassius Marcellus Clay and a cousin of Madeline Breckinridge. Clay founded KERA after witnessing her parents' bitter divorce and her mother's lack of legal standing or recourse—and she set out to right those wrongs as she saw them. She helped secure an 1890 legislative act giving married women control over their own wages. Subsequent laws were passed granting women equal property rights and the right to be co-guardians of their children. But politicians drew the line at women's suffrage. "I love them too much to allow them to vote," said a delegate to the 1890 state constitutional convention.

KERA lobbied the legislature every year to gain the right to vote in school elections, gradually tying their efforts to the educational reform movement gathering momentum at the time. Familiarly, Kentucky public education of the day was poorly funded and little teacher training was offered. Illiteracy was high.

Breckinridge was working at the time as legislative chairwoman of the Kentucky Federation of Women's Clubs when she began to see voting as the cure of a variety of societal ills. All-male government was slow or unwilling to respond to the need for reforms in health, education and charity, a reluctance she thought would change if females were added to their constituencies. So in 1908, Breckinridge's federation joined with Clay's KERA to seek complete voting rights—women's suffrage—as their ultimate goal. They began with another school suffrage fight, one they lost.

TURNING TIDE

But the tide was turning by 1912, when Breckinridge began arguing strongly that women could change Kentucky's dismal education system and a reputed 12 percent illiteracy rate. The question, she said, "seems to be not whether women are fit for school suffrage but whether men are fit for it." In an increasingly intense political climate, the Kentucky General Assembly voted nearly two to one in favor of granting all literate women the right to vote in school elections.

In the wake of this success, Clay stepped down as KERA president in favor of her more youthful cousin. Breckinridge breathed new life into the organization, expanding its membership through active recruitment and such things as essay contests, suffrage hikes, parades, automobile trips and tents at county fairs. Membership skyrocketed from 1,779 members in 1912 to more than 15,000 three years later.

An excellent writer and public speaker—often compared to her great-grandfather Henry Clay—Breckinridge used her abilities to publicize the suffrage movement wherever she could, especially in the *Lexington Herald*, which was edited and published by her husband, Desha Breckinridge.

In 1913, while testifying before a U.S. House of Representatives committee, she pointed to the fact that male voting was limited to those over twenty-one who weren't insane or convicted felons. She said it was a shame that Kentucky women were compared "poetically with whiskey and horses" and "politically with imbeciles and criminals."

Breckinridge and Clay became the first women to address a joint session of the Kentucky legislature the following year when they argued for a full-suffrage bill, which was defeated by liquor interests fearful that women would vote for prohibition.

Laura Clay's niece, Elise Smith, became KERA president in 1916, while Breckinridge concentrated her efforts on the general assembly as the group's campaign chairwoman.

When Governor James B. McCreary tried to enlist women in a Preparedness program as World War I approached, he incurred the considerable wrath of Madeline McDowell Breckinridge: "Kentucky women are not idiots, even though they are closely related to Kentucky men," she wrote. "You can't ignore them and treat them as though they were kindergarten children, and then when work is needed expect them to do a man's share." She was also critical of many of her counterparts in the South, who "are trying to get suffrage…in the most lady-like manner, without having anybody find out they want it."

National Plan

Carrie Chapman Catt, president of the National American Woman Suffrage Association, advised the various state suffrage organizations to abandon their separate efforts in favor of her "Winning Plan" to secure a women's voting amendment to the U.S. Constitution.

Though they had high hopes that the Kentucky legislature would look favorably upon the question in its 1918 session, KERA agreed to the plan. "They will never know what they asked us to give up," Breckinridge lamented. But the Winning Plan worked.

World War I brought women into nontraditional jobs to replace men fighting in France. President Woodrow Wilson was converted to the suffrage cause and politicians began seeing suffragists less as radicals and more as potential voters.

The U.S. House of Representatives passed the so-called Susan B. Anthony amendment and the Senate approved on June 4, 1919, beginning the long fight to secure ratification by the legislatures of three-fourths of the states. Kentucky Republicans generally supported the amendment, and many Democrats were swayed by President Wilson's conversion. As a result, both parties' platforms supported women's suffrage in the 1919 gubernatorial election, which was won by Somerset Republican Edwin Porch Morrow.

Kentucky Ratifies

Newly reinstalled as KERA president, Breckinridge went to work to secure Kentucky's ratification of the amendment. She launched her

Suffragists, including Madeline McDowell Breckinridge and Laura Clay, posed in Lexington in the early part of the 1900s. *Courtesy of Special Collections & Archives, University of Kentucky.*

Madeline McDowell Breckinridge and other suffragists were present on January 6, 1920, when Governor Edwin Porch Morrow signed Kentucky's ratification of the Nineteenth Amendment, which guarantees women the right to vote. *Courtesy Special Collections & Archives, University of Kentucky.*

campaign in Pikeville on July 4, 1919, and worked her way across the state, lobbying every member of the general assembly.

Her results varied. "Yes I believe in suffrage," one legislator wrote. "My mother taught me that 50 years ago…I believe in women doing anything they want to do. It is none of my business and besides many of them have got as much or more sense that I have."

"The American woman is the most adorable creature of God," wrote Dr. H.T. Morris. "But I do not believe in the principle of woman suffrage."

But Breckinridge had the support of Governor Morrow, whose cousin, Christine Bradley South, was a former KERA president, and all signs pointed to ratification.

On January 6, 1920—the usually ceremonial first day of the legislative session—Breckinridge went to Frankfort to witness the vote. The amendment passed both houses of the legislature by substantial margins. Breckinridge, South and the women of KERA gathered in Governor Morrow's office to witness his signing of the ratification, making Kentucky the twenty-fourth state to approve what would become the Nineteenth Amendment, which guarantees women the right to vote.

Jubilant, KERA's president began planning the group's conversion to a League of Women Voters. She cast her first ballot in November, voting in the 1920 presidential election. Two weeks later—on Thanksgiving Day—Madeline McDowell Breckinridge died of a stroke she had suffered on November 23. She was forty-eight years old.

Tommy Gun

Among the very few Americans to see Teddy Roosevelt and his Rough Riders charge up Kettle Hill in the San Juan Heights of Cuba in 1898 was a Kentuckian, John Taliaferro Thompson of Newport. Unlike most of his countrymen, however, Thompson was not thrilled by the sight. In fact, he was frightened and disgusted. These U.S. Volunteers, armed with 1860s-era Springfield rifles and smoky black gunpowder, had been forced to overcome the superior firepower of their Spanish opponents, who were equipped with Mauser repeating rifles, Maxim machine guns and smokeless ammunition.

Thompson's concern was derived from his job as the army's chief ordnance officer, the man in charge of equipping the Americans. The only bright spot, it seemed to Lieutenant Colonel Thompson, was the Gatling gun, capable of firing rapidly to great effect. Nevertheless, the gun was a large, nearly immobile field piece that required two soldiers to operate.

A born inventor, Thompson began to envision a small, hand-held machine gun, one that could put the Gatling's firepower into the hands of each American soldier and, perhaps, make war obsolete in the process.

West Point Heritage

Born December 31, 1860, in Newport, in a house overlooking Cincinnati, Thompson was the son of Lieutenant Colonel James Thompson, a West Point graduate and Civil War veteran. His mother, Julia Maria Taliaferro, was a polished woman of prominent and well-documented genealogy. After following in his father's footsteps to the U.S. Military Academy and the U.S. Army, Thompson was an expert in small arms by the time he found himself overseeing munitions shipments and observing the battles of the Spanish-American War.

Despite his five-foot, seven-inch height, he was described as "strongly built" and "soldierly," with an enthusiastic personality. Observers noted his inventiveness, an "imaginative quality, by which he is able to project his thoughts into the future and resolve an occasion yet to arrive" and a burning desire to "improve existing conditions."

BORN INVENTOR

From 1908 to 1914, Thompson developed ideas for his gun in the Army Ordnance Department, eventually as colonel and chief of the Small Arms Division. He was the foremost military proponent of automatic weapons, which the army's leadership was slow to embrace. Older generals had a tendency to resist the emerging technology, fearing that automatic weapons would lead to trigger-happy soldiers spraying bullets and wasting ammunition.

Thompson built his reputation as developer of the legendary 1911 Colt automatic pistol, which served as the army's standard-issue sidearm for more than six decades, and the celebrated Model 1903 Springfield rifle, which was based on the Mauser. The new Springfield's .30-caliber cartridge, in which Thompson also had a hand, became the "thirty-ought-six" that remained in army use until the 1950s.

Unable, however, to persuade army leaders to accelerate the move to automatic weapons, a frustrated Thompson resigned in November 1914 to develop and build them independently.

SUBMACHINE GUN INVENTOR

He became chief engineer at Remington Army Corp., where he designed the then-largest rifle manufacturing plant in the world, in Chester, Pennsylvania. By 1916, Thompson's ideas were ready for practical application. He founded Auto-Ordnance Corp. with his son, Captain Marcellus H. Thompson, New York financier Thomas Fortune Ryan and Captain John Bell Blish. Blish, while in the navy in 1906, had developed a method of quick-loading naval guns using built-up gases in the muzzle of a gun to expel spent cartridges. Blish provided his invention, known as the Blish Lock, in exchange for stock in the company.

Thompson assembled a staff of engineers and set them to work developing a light, dependable, semiautomatic rifle. When his chief engineer reported that the .45-caliber bullet used in standard army pistols was the only cartridge that worked with the Blish Lock, Thompson decided to pursue a small, hand-held version, which he dubbed a "submachine" gun.

"Trench Broom"

World War I, with its trench-warfare stalemates and mustard gas, was in full swing during this time, and Thompson reentered the army as director of arsenals. He oversaw small arms production, winning the Distinguished Service Medal and a promotion to brigadier general.

In the meantime, Auto-Ordnance's new submachine gun was ready for testing. Weighing twelve pounds fully loaded, it fired like a machine gun, but was maneuverable and easy to reload. It could fire twenty rounds in less than one second and was dubbed Annihilator One. Thompson called it a "trench broom," perfect for sweeping the enemy from its trenches. Several hundred prototypes were manufactured for use by army units. They were shipped on November 11, 1918, the day World War I officially ended.

Sales Fizzle

His largest potential customer thus eliminated, Thompson turned to police forces. In his capacity as vice-president of sales, the inventor marketed the gun's effectiveness and light weight. "This weapon changes the odds, which are now against the officers of the law," Thompson said during a demonstration of his gun. "[It] gives them instead a decided advantage over the bandits. Any man will think twice before going up against one."

The spectators at these events, often military officers, municipal officials and reporters, were dazzled by the weapon, which could by then fire up to 1,500 rounds per minute. Thompson once put his gun into the hands of three police officers and told each to shoot at an unoccupied nearby sedan. "The three guns, pounding out steel-jacketed .45 caliber bullets at the rate of 1,000 per minute, sliced the tires off the machine, cut through the body, radiator, lamps, steering gear, tanks and woodwork," wrote a reporter from the *New York Herald*. "The bullets converted a solid-looking, seven-passenger touring car into a flaming mass of junk in less than a minute," he wrote. "Nothing larger than a mouse could have survived the fusillade."

Buoyed by the good reviews—and favorable trials—Thompson contracted with Colt to manufacture fifteen thousand guns and sent his salesmen to police forces and military units throughout the United States and Europe.

Sales were abysmal. A Thompson with a one-hundred-shot drum magazine cost $220, a .45-caliber pistol $17.50. Customers couldn't see a practical use for such firepower, leaving the inventor with a product in search of a need. Thompson turned to the American public and began marketing the gun for use on ranches and for home protection. They were often sold by hardware stores.

GANGSTERS' FAVORITE

One Chicago storeowner rented guns to young gangsters and didn't ask questions when they were returned still warm. When he added a Thompson to his stock, it became enormously popular with the hoodlums, who valued its small size and firepower. It could easily be concealed and was accurate at a distance, even when fired from a moving car. Gangsters and outlaws used it for their murderous "hits" or the multitude of Depression-era robberies, and its fame spread, much to the horror of the gun's inventor.

George "Machine Gun" Kelly's notorious career began when his wife bought him a Thompson at a pawn shop. "Pretty Boy" Floyd removed the butt stock and fore grip from his Thompson and used it as a more easily concealed machine-pistol.

The gun was called "a diabolical engine of Death." Mobsters dubbed it a chopper, Chicago typewriter or—in macabre homage to Thompson—a "Tommy gun."

The first gangland "hit" with a Thompson was reported in Chicago in the fall of 1925. On February 14, 1929, Al Capone had his henchmen line up seven rival bootleggers against a wall and machine-gun them to death, in what came to be known as the St. Valentine's Day Massacre.

ARMS RACE

Awakened by the carnage, city police departments inundated Auto-Ordnance with orders. FBI Director J. Edgar Hoover authorized his agents to carry

Newport's John T. Thompson had hoped to invent a weapon to ensure world peace. Instead, it was used by 1920s Chicago gangsters to settle their scores. The Thompson, or Tommy gun, as it was known, later helped the Allies win World War II. *Courtesy of the Library of Congress.*

Thompsons, and Melvin Purvis, agent in charge of the Chicago FBI office, required his agents to gain proficiency with the weapon. The federal government acted to keep the Thompson out of criminal hands. The Gun Control Act of 1934 prohibited the public sale or possession of the gun, punishable by ten years in prison and a $10,000 fine.

Hollywood, reacting to the bloody gangland wars, began churning out gangster movies, turning actors like James Cagney, Edward G. Robinson, George Raft and Humphrey Bogart into stars overnight.

The gun Thompson had hoped to make famous had become infamous.

"I have given my valedictory to arms, as I want to pay more attention now to saving human life than destroying it," the anguished inventor wrote. "May the deadly [gun] always speak for God & Country. It has worried me that the gun has been so stolen by evil men & used for purposes outside our motto, 'On the side of law and order.'"

WORLD WAR II

Though its product was beginning to gain acceptance by federal law enforcement agencies and the armed forces, Auto-Ordnance still hadn't sold all of its original inventory of fifteen thousand 1921 models—and the company was in precarious financial standing.

Germany's 1939 invasion of Poland shocked France into ordering three thousand Thompsons, and Britain ordered more. The U.S. military adopted the weapon for use by paratroopers. Solvent again, Auto-Ordnance built a new plant in Bridgeport, Connecticut, and began filling orders for updated military versions of the gun.

Just when his brainchild had begun to live down its notorious reputation, Thompson died of heart failure at his New York home on June 21, 1940. New company President Russell McGuire directed efforts to get Thompsons into the hands of American soldiers.

The new Thompson became available in late 1942 and was used by every branch of service and every ally during the war, both in Europe and the Pacific. More than 1.2 million were purchased between 1942 and 1945. Soldiers hailed their maneuverability and accuracy. Some became so proficient with the gun that they could reputedly write their names in bullet holes. The Thompson is said to have terrorized German troops, who were known to retreat upon hearing its distinctive sound.

MODERN ERA

John Taliaferro Thompson's weapon continued to help protect American troops in Korea and Vietnam, and the FBI didn't phase out its use until the 1970s. The Thompson submachine gun's legend today lives on in gangster movies and among collectors, who reportedly are known to pay more than $10,000 for particularly good models in mint condition.

Unlike his successors at Auto-Ordnance, Thompson never made a fortune from his invention. His contribution did, however, aid soldiers in battle and make police safer on the streets.

A magazine article called the Kentuckian's career "a magnificent piece of work—one that will stand [as] a monument to the constructive genius and industrious application of Thompson long after he has passed away. Such a man is a very great credit to the soil which produced him."

Was Hot Lips a Kentuckian?

By the end of its eleven-year run, the TV show *M*A*S*H* had developed almost a cult-like following among millions of its fans. In fact, its last episode, in 1983, was watched by 125 million people, making it the highest-rated program in television history.

Anyone who remembers *M*A*S*H* will recall terms like "bugging out," the sister mobile hospital known as the 8055th—or Eight-O-double-nickel—and of course the passionate, if somewhat dysfunctional, courtship between head nurse Major Margaret "Hot Lips" Houlihan and her married boyfriend, Major Frank Burns.

But *M*A*S*H* was more than a TV program; it was a tribute to the real people who pioneered a new medical concept that saved countless lives in the Korean and Vietnam Wars, and which continues to this day in Iraq and Afghanistan.

Among the real people involved in the history of Mobile Army Surgical Hospitals was an army nurse named Lieutenant Lelia Jeanette Jones of Irvine, in Estill County. Born in 1921 as one of the six children of Henry and Elizabeth (Williams) Jones, Lelia was described as feisty and full of fight, despite her five-foot, three-inch height.

Lelia's brother H.C. joined the service in World War II, and she began nursing training in Middletown, Ohio. The family received word that H.C. was reported missing in action on April 9, 1943. Lelia applied to join the Army Nurse Corps eleven days later, on April 20. Initially rejected for being underweight, she solved the problem by eating bananas.

JOINING UP

Lelia finally became an army nurse on March 10, 1945, as the war was winding down, and worked at stateside hospitals—including at Fort Knox and in Richmond—almost until the Korean War began in 1950. Her arrival in Korea quickly became a baptism by fire. She landed in Pusan, the southernmost city in Korea, the day before the South Korean capital, Seoul, fell to Chinese Communist forces. Assigned to the Fourteenth U.S. Army Field Hospital, Lieutenant Jones helped set up a hospital for prisoner of war wounded. The hospital quickly had 10,500 patients, making it one of the largest in the world.

In early 1951, American forces under Lieutenant General Matthew B. Ridgway counterattacked, and the front lines stabilized near the 38th Parallel, which would become the permanent boundary of North and South Korea. After being hospitalized in Tokyo for a respiratory ailment that would plague her for the remainder of her life, the newly promoted Captain Lelia Jones was ordered to report to the 8055th M*A*S*H at Uijongbu, Korea, in July.

MASH

The 8055th was the army's pioneer mobile surgical hospital, a new concept designed to treat soldiers' wounds as quickly as possible and send the wounded to more specialized care in Tokyo or the United States. Helicopters brought the wounded from the battlefield to the MASH, usually placed about twenty miles behind the front lines. Doctors performed "meatball surgery," quickly solving a patient's most life-threatening problem, and then moved him out.

Dr. H. Richard Hornberger, a surgeon assigned to the Double Nickel, described the method: "We are not concerned with the ultimate reconstruction of the patient. We are concerned only with getting the kid out of here alive enough for someone else to reconstruct him."

Much depicted in the television show had a basis in reality. Nurses and doctors worked twelve-hour shifts in combat conditions, living in tents and wearing helmets virtually every waking hour. It was standard procedure among the nurses during the brutal Korean winters to sleep in thermal underwear, flannel pajamas, a sweater, stockings, gloves and a surgical "stockinette" on their heads. Then, they slipped inside a sleeping bag and pulled several layers of blankets over them.

Much more than just another pretty face, Estill County native Lelia Busler saved countless lives as a nurse in the MASH units of Korea. She was forced to retire from service in 1973 due to health issues, but not before a promotion to the rank of colonel and being awarded the army's Legion of Merit and Medical Department medal. *Courtesy of John Trowbridge.*

As the battles of Punchbowl, Old Baldy, Bloody Ridge and Heartbreak Ridge raged, the Double Nickel fought to save the lives of the casualties brought there, a number that reached thirty thousand the month of Lelia's arrival.

PULLING RANK

General Ridgway was a proponent of the surgical hospital concept, and often visited his wounded soldiers. Known for his aggressive nature and habit of hanging live grenades on the front of his uniform, the general arrived at the Double Nickel on a day when Captain Lelia Jones was in charge of the pre-op ward.

Because MASHs treated soldiers of both sides, it was a violation of army procedure to possess loaded weapons or munitions within their wards. When Ridgway attempted to walk into pre-op, Captain Jones stepped in front of him, informing the commanding general that she would not allow him inside unless he removed his grenades and secured his pistol. Ridgway wordlessly gave the offending items to an aide and continued his tour.

Nurse Frances Barnes of Tuscaloosa, Alabama, whose tour at the 8055th almost exactly mirrored that of Lelia Jones, remembered her friend and colleague in her 2000 book *Memoirs of an Army MASH Nurse in Korea*:

> *Lelia, or "Little Bit," was an excellent, devoted nurse. She could be moody at times, but usually liked to talk. A beautiful woman with curly, brown hair and hazel eyes that were striking, you noticed her eyes right away. She had a great figure even in the fatigues that we wore every day. She was the only woman stationed at the MASH who did not wear a bra, she was a decade ahead of her time. A southern woman who oozed charm and gentility when she had a mind to, she let you know right away what she thought about something.*

AN AFFAIR

Barnes also recalled Jones's hush-hush affair with a married army doctor, a romance that did not survive the war.

Between battles, or when truce negotiations were underway, things got a little wacky when the men and women of the 8055th blew off the steam of their stressful service. They played baseball, horseshoes and volleyball and, in the summer, swam in "clear pools formed by mountain streams." When asked about his activities during those times, Hornberger said, "Oh sex and liquor. What else is there?"

Jones left the Double Nickel in January 1952, returning back home to Kentucky, where she worked at the Fort Campbell Hospital. In a twenty-eight-year army career, she moved from the Panama Canal Zone to Puerto Rico and Germany to, once again, Korea. She married and divorced, and was regularly promoted.

A colonel by 1973, Lelia Jones Busler, just on the verge of a command of her own, began suffering from COPD, or chronic obstructive pulmonary disease, a smoker's ailment that was aggravated by the lung condition she had contracted in Korea. When she retired on June 30 of that year, her superior officer, Colonel Arthur W. Buswell, wrote of her: "If she chose to remain on active duty, she has the understanding, knowledge, and ability to become the ultimate Chief, of the Army Nurse Corps."

As she left the service, Colonel Busler was awarded the army's Legion of Merit and Medical Department medals.

Retirement

Returning home, Lelia settled in Richmond, near her sister and brother-in-law, Anna and Tom Etherington. She volunteered at a religious bookstore and spent her Sundays at Christ Episcopal Church.

As her health worsened, she became dependent on bottled oxygen and the medication she took weakened her bones. Busler fell and broke a hip in 1980 and, while a patient at the Veterans Administration Hospital in Lexington, died on May 29, 1981. She was buried with her family in West Irvine Cemetery.

There is no question that Colonel Lelia Jeanette Jones Busler served her country well in the worst of conditions and over nearly three decades. But was she the inspiration for "Hot Lips" Houlihan? The facts point in that direction.

"Feisty," outspoken and strong-willed—and known for her romance with a married doctor—she had served in the 8055th with Captain H. Richard Hornberger. Writing as Richard Hooker, it was Hornberger's 1968 novel that was the basis for the movie that became the TV series *M*A*S*H*.

About the Author

Photo by Sean T. Stephens.

Tom Stephens, senior correspondent and history columnist for *Kentucky Monthly* magazine, has been a published historical writer for more than two decades. His work has appeared in *Louisville* magazine, the *Lexington Herald-Leader*, *The Register of the Kentucky Historical Society*, the *American National Biography* series, the *African American National Biography*, the *Historical Dictionary of the Gilded Age* and *The Encyclopedia of Louisville*. His first book, *First Cats: Amazing Origins of the UK Sports Tradition*, published in 2005, won the Historical Confederation of Kentucky's 2005 History Award Stephens's work also has won awards from the Kentucky Association of Government Communicators, the Kentucky Press Association and the Society of Professional Journalists.